Strategies for the Threshold #9

Dealing with Kronos:
Spirit of Abuse and Time

Anne Hamilton

Janice Speirs

Dealing with Kronos: Spirit of Abuse and Time

Strategies for the Threshold #9

© Anne Hamilton and Janice Speirs 2022

Published by Armour Books

P. O. Box 492, Corinda QLD 4075

Cover Images: © allanswart 'A line of half buried antique clocks with a glass backing in a sandy desert landscape' | iStock;
© D-Keine 'Grim Reaper walking in fog. Halloween' | iStock;
© iloveotto 'Asia style textures and backgrounds' | canstockphoto.com;
© Diego Passadori 'Brown wooden surface' | Unsplash.com

Interior Design and Typeset by Beckon Creative

ISBN: 978-1-925380-49-1

 A catalogue record for this book is available from the National Library of Australia

All rights reserved. No part of this publication may be reproduced, stored in, or introduced into a retrieval system, or transmitted, in any form, or by any means (electronic, mechanical, photocopying, recording or otherwise) without the prior written permission of the publisher.

Note: Australian spelling and grammar conventions are used throughout this book.

Strategies for the Threshold #9

Dealing with Kronos:
Spirit of Abuse and Time

Anne Hamilton

Janice Speirs

Unless otherwise noted, Scripture quotations are taken from the Holy Bible, New International Version®, NIV®. Copyright © 1973, 1978, 1984, 2011 by Biblica, Inc.™ Used by permission of Zondervan. All rights reserved worldwide. www.zondervan.com The "NIV" and "New International Version" are trademarks registered in the United States Patent and Trademark Office by Biblica, Inc.™.

Scripture quotations marked AMP are taken from the Amplified Version of the Bible Copyright © 2015 by The Lockman Foundation, La Habra, CA 90631. All rights reserved. www.lockman.org

Scripture quotations marked BLB are taken from The Blue Letter Bible. Used by permission. blueletterbible.org

Scripture quotations marked BSB are taken from The Holy Bible, Berean Study Bible, BSB Copyright ©2016 by Bible Hub Used by Permission. All Rights Reserved Worldwide.

Scripture quotations marked CEV are from the Contemporary English Version Copyright © 1991, 1992, 1995 by American Bible Society. Used by Permission.

Scripture quotations marked ESV are taken from the ESV® Bible (The Holy Bible, English Standard Version®), copyright © 2001 by Crossway, a publishing ministry of Good News Publishers. Used by permission. All rights reserved.

Scripture quotations marked GNT are from the Good News Translation in Today's English Version—Second Edition Copyright © 1992 by American Bible Society. Used by Permission.

Scripture quotations marked HCSB are taken from the Holman Christian Standard Bible®, Used by Permission HCSB ©1999,2000,2002,2003,2009 Holman Bible Publishers. Holman Christian Standard Bible®, Holman CSB®, and HCSB® are federally registered trademarks of Holman Bible Publishers.

Scripture quotations marked ISV are taken from the Holy Bible: International Standard Version®. Copyright © 1996-forever by The ISV Foundation. ALL RIGHTS RESERVED INTERNATIONALLY. Used by permission.

Scripture quotations marked NASB are taken from the New American Standard Bible®, Copyright © 1960, 1962, 1963, 1968, 1971, 1972, 1973, 1975, 1977, 1995 by The Lockman Foundation. Used by permission. (www.Lockman.org)

Scripture quotations marked NLT are taken from the Holy Bible, New Living Translation, copyright 1996, 2004. Used by permission of Tyndale House Publishers, Inc., Wheaton, Illinois 60189. All rights reserved.

Scripture quotations marked NIV are taken from the Holy Bible, New International Version®, NIV®. Copyright © 1973, 1978, 1984, 2011 by Biblica, Inc.™ Used by permission of Zondervan. All rights reserved worldwide. www.zondervan.com The "NIV" and "New International Version" are trademarks registered in the United States Patent and Trademark Office by Biblica, Inc.™.

Scripture quotations marked NKJV are taken from the New King James Version. Copyright © 1982 by Thomas Nelson, Inc. Used by permission. All rights reserved.

Scripture quotations marked NRS are taken from New Revised Standard Version of the Bible, copyright 1952 [2nd edition, 1971] by the Division of Christian Education of the National Council of the Churches of Christ in the United States of America. Used by permission. All rights reserved.

Scripture quotations marked PHPS are taken from the New Testament in Modern English © 1958, 1959, 1960 J.B. Phillips and 1947, 1952, 1955, 1957 The Macmillan Company, New York. Used by permission. All rights reserved.

Other Books By Anne Hamilton

In this series

Dealing with Python: Spirit of Constriction
(with *Arpana Dev Sangamithra*)

Dealing with Ziz: Spirit of Forgetting

Name Covenant: Invitation to Friendship

Hidden in the Cleft: True and False Refuge

Dealing with Leviathan: Spirit of Retaliation

Dealing with Resheph: Spirit of Trouble
(with *Irenie Senior*)

Dealing with Azazel: Spirit of Rejection

Dealing with Belial: Spirit of Armies and Abuse
(with *Janice Speirs*)

Devotional Theology series

God's Poetry: The Identity & Destiny Encoded in Your Name

God's Panoply: The Armour of God & the Kiss of Heaven

God's Pageantry: The Threshold Guardians
& the Covenant Defender

God's Pottery: The Sea of Names & the Pierced Inheritance

God's Priority: World-Mending & Generational Testing

More Precious than Pearls (with *Natalie Tensen*)

As Resplendent As Rubies (with *Natalie Tensen*)

As Exceptional as Sapphires (with *Donna Ho*)

Spiritual Legal Rights (with *Janice Sergison*)

Jesus and the Healing of History Series

1 *Like Wildflowers, Suddenly*
2 *Bent World, Bright Wings*
3 *Silk Shadows, Rings of Gold*
4 *Where His Feet Pass*
5 *The Singing Silence*

Contents

Introduction		9
1	**The Council of Heaven**	13
	Prayer	37
2	**Except God Alone**	41
	Prayer	66
3	**Turn Back Time**	69
	Prayer	105
4	**The Ancient of Days**	107
	Prayer	138
5	**Fruit That Lasts**	141
	Prayer	170
6	**The Garden Beyond Time**	173
	Prayer	191
7	**Timely and Untimely**	193
	Prayer	221
Appendix 1	Summary	225
Appendix 2	Additional Prayers	231
Endnotes		239

Introduction

ABOUT AN HOUR AFTER I FINISHED the previous book in this series, as I was relaxing with a cup of coffee, I had a nudge from the Holy Spirit to check out the precise Hebrew wording in the story of Abraham's test at Mount Moriah.

Now I wasn't planning on starting a new book within hours of completing *Dealing with Belial*. But that's what happened. At first, the clues God handed me were a gift—much, I felt, like, 'Well done, good and faithful servant and here's some more!'—but very quickly I started to feel intense spiritual pressure to get a move on with this companion volume.

Now my motto comes from Isaiah 28:16, *'Those who believe will not be in haste,'* and hurrying is not my usual style. I can wait twenty years for a revelation of what's wrong with a book I'm writing. And I've done just that—known something was wrong but not what or how to fix it—so I've just waited on the Lord until the answer became evident. And that's been decades in more than one instance. Rushing? No.

But an insistent compulsion to get this particular book out as soon as possible prevailed. And perhaps because so much of it is about the untimely delays that some of our Scriptural heroes were prone to, it was wise to yield to the pressure and not procrastinate. Still I'm genuinely hoping that, an hour from now, I'll be having a lovely chat with the Lord, enjoying coffee, but minus any new revelation.

First, a huge **thank you** to Janice for her invaluable contribution.

Second, as usual, there are some disclaimers. This is not the last word on the topic of the spirit of abuse, just an ongoing part of the dialogue. It's not even a comprehensive overview of Kronos because I wanted to focus on the monumental miracles of God in relation to Time. It's a follow-up to *Dealing with Belial* and many statements made here, without supporting evidence or argument, are baldly asserted because the case for them has been made in a previous book in this series.

I am a numerical literary stylist. That means the sections of text in this work all conform to the mathematical design principles found in the Word of God. I am by no means in the league of the Scripture writers who encoded musical notation and numerical symbolism in their work but, at an incredibly basic kindergarten level, I have employed this ancient artform throughout this book. And I hope it's so deeply integrated into the writing that you never even notice it is there!

Anne Hamilton
Bastille Day 2022

1

The Council of Heaven

ONE WET SUNDAY MORNING in the last quarter of the last century, I was moaning to God as I drove to church. The topic of my complaint was, unsurprisingly, money. I'd helped to organise a conference—an event that had, in fact, been extremely successful... except on the financial side.

The week before the conference we'd been tracking well with the bookings and also the projected attendance. Financially, we were about three-quarters of the way towards our break-even point. Since we knew that, as a general rule, twice as many people actually turned up on the day as had pre-registered, the committee felt quite confident about the outcome.

What none of us had counted on was a forty-eight hour deluge of torrential rain immediately before the start of the conference. Roads were cut, power was out, bridges were under water. When we arrived at the venue via an extremely circuitous back route, we discovered a waterfall in one of the conference rooms. Instead of floods of conference delegates, there were floods of the watery kind.

Those of us who actually made it there had a wonderful time. But, as one of the coordinators, I was responsible for the financial mop-up. My share was going to amount to a few thousand dollars. It could have been far worse, but I was still disappointed. 'I checked with You so many times,' I told God that Sunday morning, the following week. 'I thought You said this was right. I thought You were going to protect us financially. I don't know how I'm going to afford this.'

'If you knew what we were up against,' He replied, 'you'd think this was a very good outcome.'

'So what? Aren't You God? What do You mean: *"what we were up against"*?' I was stunned. I tried to make sense of what I'd just heard but I had no theological grid to put it in.

Now I don't always hear the voice of God loud and clear but that particular morning He was coming through in high-definition fidelity sound. Yet I was totally baffled. 'What has any enemy got to do with this?' I asked. 'Is anything too hard for You? Aren't You, you know, all-knowing, all-powerful, almighty... omnipotent, omniscient, omnipresent... all those 'omni' words?'

'It's complicated.'

It was fortunate I didn't have anything to choke on at that point. 'Complicated!? What do you mean "complicated"?'

I tried to process the word. *What,* I wondered, *could possibly be 'complicated' for God?*

'Answer coming up in the next five minutes.'

Once I'd heard that, I was on high alert as I arrived at church and the service began. One of the readings[1] for that day was Psalm 82. The opening verse is iconoclastic, theology-shattering:

> *God has stood up in the council of heaven: in the midst of the gods He gives judgment.*
> *'How long will you judge unjustly: and favour the cause of the wicked?*
> *Judge for the poor and fatherless: vindicate the afflicted and oppressed.*
> *Rescue the poor and needy: and save them from the hands of the wicked.*
> *They do not know, they do not understand, they walk about in darkness:*
> *all the foundations of the earth are shaken.*
> *Therefore I say, "Though you are gods: and all of you children of the Most High,*
> *Nevertheless you shall die like a mortal: and fall like one of the princes."'*
> *Arise, O God, and judge the earth:*
> *for You shall take all nations as Your possession.*

I knew immediately it was God's answer. My spirit resonated with it: *God has stood up in the council of heaven: in the midst of the gods He gives judgment.* But that's not to say I understood it. What on earth, I asked myself, does that first verse mean?

When I went home, I typed out the Psalm and taped it next to my computer, where it stayed for years as I wrestled with it. Over time, I realised God had indeed been right about a 'very good outcome'. I watched other people organise very similar conferences and go down financially: thirty thousand dollars, fifty thousand dollars and, in one spectacular disaster, a quarter of a million dollars. Clearly, whatever we were 'up against' was formidable. Very formidable.

'So what?' That had been my first question in reply to God's comment and it remained unanswered for years. What did it actually matter how formidable the enemy was? Where was God's protection in all this? Why was it, according to God's own testimony—if I'd heard right—*'complicated'*?

It was only when I started to come to terms with the existence of angelic sentinels who watch over thresholds—fallen throne guardians[2]—that I began to make real sense of that description, 'complicated'. Until the moment that I realised that both holy and unholy angels watch over transitions in space and time, I didn't get 'what we were up against.' But then it became obvious that, from the cherubim guarding the entrance to Eden with their whirling swords to the angel who left Peter after escorting him through the iron gates of the city, God's attendants are found at both physical and spiritual doorways.

At first, rather naïvely, I thought that there were just three supernatural sentries who guarded thresholds—Python, Rachab and Leviathan. The constrictor, the waster and the retaliator. It shouldn't take too long to find the Scriptures pertaining to them—so I thought.

I started to look into their tactics because, while it may have been true that, back in Paul's day, believers were not ignorant of the satan's devices, it certainly wasn't so today. And, somewhat selfishly I admit—because I simply didn't want to lose money coordinating another conference—I wanted to know what their spiritual legal rights were. I was willing to accept that God did not intervene on my behalf, but that suggested to me there was some unresolved sin or possibly iniquity—generational transgression—that needed removal through the application of the Cross of Jesus. In addition, of course, I wanted to be able to recognise their tactics and agendas, so I would not be caught unawares in the future.

Now, during this time, I had another conversation with God—actually, He was upbraiding me about my resistance to His will—when He happened to mention His 'divine council'. That was a term I thought I recognised. It was surely simply another way of saying 'council of heaven'. But because God had been urging me to stop struggling against His calling for me, I thought I'd check it out. And the timing was absolutely perfect for a google search. Because there, in the top results, was a link to a seminar on the 'divine council' the following week in a city just two hours away. I booked in right then and there.

During the seminar itself, I was chatting with others during a coffee break, when it suddenly dawned on me that I'd crashed a semi-private gathering. There were lots of questions about who I was, what I was doing there, how I'd discovered the existence of the group and how I managed to book in to the seminar. I got the distinct impression the organisers thought I was some sort of spy, there to gather dirt on their religious orthodoxy, or lack thereof. I tried to explain that I'd heard the words 'divine council' in a conversation with God and just googled up their seminar, along with the date, time and place, but that did not seem remotely credible to them. Although they believed in such a mode of revelation, they simply couldn't credit that God would send someone as 'normal' and 'ordinary' as me to their meeting. I wasn't, in their view, the type of person who hears from God.

I mention all this background because I want you to know that my interest in the Divine Council is not an academic one. It was birthed in the challenges and frustrations of everyday life. It toddled along, getting to its feet through an encounter with the work of Tom Hawkins who specialised in helping people afflicted by ritual abuse. In his mind-wowing *Cosmic Hierarchy and Appeal to the Heavenly Court*,[3] he mentioned that the theological background behind his work was that of Michael Heiser.

Sooner or later, if you're looking for material to understand the Divine Council, you'll run into Michael Heiser's contributions. These days, it's very much sooner, rather than later. Heiser is the premier scholar currently promoting what is now widely termed the 'Divine Council Worldview'. Not surprisingly, he credits his present understanding to a mind-melting encounter with the text of that first verse of Psalm 82. There's no escaping it, as he discovered on examining the Hebrew grammar: God does indeed stand up in the assembly of the gods.

That's a shot amidships to monotheism as it's developed in the last century or so.

God [elohim] *has stood up in the council of heaven: in the midst of the gods* [elohim] *He gives judgement.*

See the problem? Same word, different translation. Michael Heiser explores the text in great detail and reveals the various theological gymnastics that scholars have tried in an effort to wriggle out of the implications. Some suggest that the Hebrew word, 'elohim', doesn't mean *gods* at all, at least in this context, but *judges*. However, that then makes nonsense of the rest of the psalm. Judges don't need to be told they'll die like humanity; they know it already because they're decidedly human. A prophetic declaration about dying like mortals is only a threat to a supernatural being who has no reason to suspect that corruption and injustice could actually affect its existence by changing its status of immortality.

In addition, it creates a real difficulty with the sixth verse:

> *I have said, 'You are gods* [elohim]; *you are all sons of the Most High.'*

Psalm 82:6 BSB

If 'elohim' here is really *judges*, it contradicts what Jesus says when He quotes this verse in John 10:34. Jesus didn't use *judges* there, He used *gods*. In fact, His argument with the Jewish leaders entirely relies on this verse saying and meaning *'gods'*.

Now Psalm 82 is not the only Scripture to discuss or portray the Divine Council, so even if we sweep it under that bulging rug where the hard sayings of Scripture are hidden from sight, the issue doesn't go away. For example, there's Psalm 89:

> *For who in the skies can be compared to the Lord? Who among the heavenly beings is like the Lord, a God greatly to be feared in the council of the holy ones, and awesome above all who are around Him?*

Psalm 89:6–7 ESV

And, of course, there's the opening to the Book of Job. The heavenly hosts present themselves to God and the satan takes the opportunity to visit the court, answer vaguely in response to a question about his activities, before going on to challenge God's statements about the uprightness of Job. This scene where Job, unbeknownst to himself, is appointed God's designated champion takes place within the Divine Council.

In a similar vein, what can we make of the vision of Micaiah, who told King Ahab:

> *I saw the Lord sitting on His throne, and all the host of heaven standing by Him on His right and on His left.*
>
> *And the Lord said, 'Who will entice Ahab to march up and fall at Ramoth-gilead?'*
>
> *And one suggested this, and another that. Then a spirit came forward, stood before the Lord, and said, 'I will entice him.'*
>
> *'By what means?' asked the Lord.*
>
> *And he replied, 'I will go out and be a lying spirit in the mouths of all his prophets.'*
>
> *'You will surely entice him and prevail,' said the Lord. 'Go and do it.'*
>
> 1 Kings 22:19–22 BSB

That's a fairly disturbing passage, isn't it? Since Micaiah's announcement of his vision takes place on the threshing floor at the gate of Samaria, and since it prophesies the end of a king's reign, the scene has all the marks of a threshold event. That spirit is therefore almost certainly one of the throne guardians.

Later I'll have a go at unriddling this strange event in the heavenly council. To many people, the council is so far out of their theological comfort zone, something they consider so esoteric and weird, that they shut the door on it.

Apart from my selfish monetary reason for persisting in wanting to understand Psalm 82, there was another reason too. To add to my 'need to know' list, I'd experienced a strange visitation by a group of masked spiritual entities. They exuded unalloyed exuberance at some coup they'd pulled off and it felt to me, when I ever-so-briefly encountered them, they were on a holiday tour. They were as surprised I could see them as I was startled at their sudden manifestation. Initially, I thought I was having an hallucination but, as God drip-fed me information about what I'd seen and heard over the next fifteen years, I gradually came to the conclusion that what I'd seen was real, was from another realm, and was quite high in the cosmic scheme of things when it came to Paul's list of principalities, powers and world-rulers.

For many years, long before I realised it was the case, I was battling principalities and powers. Ironically, that kind of warfare was the very thing I thought I was steering clear of. I think many of us are under the misapprehension we're doing the same.

The immense value of Heiser's scholarship is that it reintroduces a supernatural worldview to the sacred text and confronts us with the deficiencies of modern monotheism. By maintaining that the ancient Israelites believed in only one deity, when Scripture testifies that 'it's complicated', many modern translations have erased the role of spirits in both the heavenly and earthly realms.

Sometimes the names of threshold guardians have been reduced to abstract qualities—such as *worthless*—or are redefined as functions—such as *fortune-telling*. Sometimes the names of these angelic princes are regarded as personifications, rather than persons in their own right.

Belial, for example, is mentioned 27 times in Hebrew, but in English has largely vanished as an entity with a complex nature. Instead it's been abstracted and tagged *worthless* or *nothing* or *wicked*. You'd never guess it was a spirit of abuse and armies and you'd entirely miss the point of the solitary reference to it in Paul's second letter to the Corinthians where, bizarrely, the majority of translations mention it by name.

Resheph, for another example, is mentioned seven times in Hebrew, but in English has gone up in a puff of *fiery sparks* or else been personified (or is it depersonified?) as *pestilence*. You'd never see that Jesus confronted Resheph on at least seven occasions. Deber, a herald of God, is transformed into *plague* at the same time as Resheph gets a makeover as *fever*.[4]

Python, likewise, has disappeared into a function—*divination* is the usual substitute for its name. Ziz, at least, has the distinction of not being reduced to something inanimate. It's variously translated as *insects*, *animals, wild beasts, everything that moves, living things, creatures, scampering mice*—but never as the Hebrew tradition pictures it: a high-ranking spirit bird.

One of the main reasons for deleting the names of these spirits is that they are the names of 'gods' in the nations around about Israel. And because there's only one God, only one Creator, only one King and Lord of all, there can't be a whole brood of little godlings, kinglets and lordlings. Except Scripture plainly says that there are.

In the nineteenth century, when theologians were fighting off the influx of comparative religion and mythology which had reduced God to, at best, 'first among equals', monotheism began to rise as a protective shield. It was unnecessary to consider the claims of other gods, past or present, if there were no other gods. But God is not 'first among equals'; He is, as Michael Heiser likes to say, species-unique. And if there are no other gods, Heiser goes on to point out, then it's nonsense to say:

> *There is no one like You among the gods, Lord.*
>
> Psalm 86:8 NASB

It's like saying: 'You're better than any non-existent being, God.' That reduces David's praise in this song to ironic mockery.

The problem, says Heiser, is largely created by the translation of the word 'elohim'. It's rendered *God* over 2300 times, and *gods* just over 200 times along with a sprinkling of *goddesses*, *rulers* and *judges*. Normally the translation is determined by the context, but as we've seen, theological pre-determination can decide the context, rather than Scripture itself.

Heiser suggests the correct translation of 'elohim' is *inhabitants of the heavenly realm*. This includes God but is not restricted to Him. The ancient Israelites thought of these beings they called 'elohim' as divine but, amongst them, Yahweh is unique. A correct understanding of how Scripture presents God is, therefore, that He is the one-and-only uncreated Creator, the only perfect and holy Most High, and the eternal Ancient of Days—*not* that He is the only 'elohim'. There are other 'elohim', other residents of heaven, inhabiting that realm with Him.

The Divine Council, the assembly of the heavenly host, is composed of 'elohim'. Some of them are Yahweh's throne guardians—four-faced whirling cherubim and fiery serpentine seraphim—who, like a king's closest equerries, are God's protectors of sacred space.[5] Some are spirits, like the wind-breath 'ruach' who volunteered to lure Ahab to his death by speaking lies through the mouths of his four hundred prophets.

But not all members of the Divine Council are 'elohim'. Some, mysteriously, are human.

> *This is what the Lord Almighty says: 'Do not listen to what the prophets are prophesying to you; they fill you with false hopes. They speak visions from their own minds, not from the mouth of the Lord ... But which of them has stood in the council of the Lord to see or to hear His word? ...*

> *I did not send these prophets, yet they have run with their message; I did not speak to them, yet they have prophesied. But if they had stood in My council, they would have proclaimed My words to My people and would have turned them from their evil ways and from their evil deeds.'*
>
> Jeremiah 23:16-22 NIV

Micaiah was present, standing in the Divine Council when he heard the Lord commission a lying spirit to entice Ahab to his death. Isaiah was present, standing in the Divine Council when he saw the Lord, high and lifted up, with His train filling the temple.

When we remove all thought of this heavenly assembly from our understanding of how God chooses to bring His plans to pass, we actually fail to see what Jesus did. Psalm 82 is a prophecy. To fulfil it Jesus had to stand up in the assembly of the gods and declare their rule at an end. He actually did this in going to the mountain where the 'assembly of El' allegedly congregated. When He came down, He sent out seventy disciples through the villages of Galilee and Samaria.

Seventy, to every Jew of the time, symbolised 'government'. Not only were there seventy members of the Sanhedrin, the ruling religious body, it was also the number associated in the Hebrew mind with the rulership of the nations. Just after the scattering from the Tower of Babel, God appointed seventy principalities to govern the world outside Israel.[6]

Jesus was constantly at war with the gods. I like to call them 'godlings' actually, so you'll often find that term here. He went up against the 'elohim' of Psalm 82. I'm making a big deal of this because, when we bundle up the thousands of references to 'elohim' as mostly an alternative name for Yahweh, we're blind to the existence of 'threshold guardians'. When we consider 'elohim' as just being the equivalent of a preferred name used by a particular scribal editor in ancient times, then 'threshold guardians' slip so far off the page they become a mythic concept derived from Joseph Campbell's study into the journey of the archetypal hero. That they are drawn directly from the record of Scripture will entirely elude us. We'll not only scrub them back to vanishing point, we'll create contradictions in the character of God that we then have to justify with a division between the Old and New Testaments.

The word 'monotheism' was coined in the seventeenth century by Henry More. Its great rise to prominence occurred in the nineteenth century, not only as a bulwark against comparative religion but, contra wise, as giving ground to evolution. The Israelites, it was thought, had a 'more evolved' religious system than their ancient neighbours, and Christianity, as the inheritors of that code, have evolved still further.

Once the supposition of religious evolution is on the table, either consciously or unconsciously, then the Bible moves from its position as a sacred text to an outdated historical document. We've shifted from divine revelation to sanctioned evolution. And there is no common ground for dialogue in those positions—one is God-centred, the other is man-centred.

Michael Heiser is keen to reintroduce the text of the Bible within its own context and milieu. That is, what did the people of the time understand by the history or the prophecy recorded for them? I don't quite share that thought-space. I want to see more than that. I want to know what Jesus did with the historical foreshadowings and prophetic declarations in His own life. Yes, I want to know what the people thought but, most importantly of all, I want to know what God thought—and thinks!

For example, the fact that, on the Day of Atonement, Jesus was at the Gates of Hell in front of a pagan shrine to a goat-human hybrid demi-god speaks clearly, as far as I am concerned, to the scapegoat ritual prescribed for that very day. Is Azazel really a 'rugged cliff' or 'utter removal' or is it, in fact, a goat deity? Once we look at the actions of Jesus, it's impossible to sideline the identification of Azazel in order to suggest it's not one of the fallen 'elohim'. Defining it as other than a supernatural entity makes no sense. The actions of Jesus do not wipe out of contention any possibility that Azazel is a former cosmic commander and ringleader in a major insurrection against God but rather place that notion front and centre.

I'm opposed to the view that, because Paul wrote post-resurrection, his words should take precedence over those of Jesus because the gospels are almost entirely pre-resurrection. If we can't harmonise the accounts, we haven't understood them. Just as many people don't realise they've given adherence to a theological system where Paul trumps Jesus, so they don't recognise their view of God's government is askew. They resist the concept of the Divine Council. Heiser's exposition is, however, more rediscovered than revolutionary.

It's important to remember the Authorised Version of the Bible, commissioned by King James, was not the first English translation of Scripture. But James didn't like any of the previous versions. His main objection was that none of them supported his philosophy of the 'divine right of kings'. Nevertheless, despite his distaste for earlier renditions, some of his authorised translators saw fit to crib from them—using words like Myles Coverdale's *lovingkindness*, invented to translate Hebrew 'chesed'.

Still, those translator-bishops knew what the king really wanted. Consequently, flowing through our English tradition of Scriptural translation and interpretation is James' slant on how royal power should be executed. God's operation of the government of heaven is so very different from what we expect because we've been unknowingly conditioned by James' views on autocracy and authority.

With all this background, I hope you are now ready and open-minded enough to consider an idea so out of the box most people might regard it as heretical. No one to blame but me for this thought. And it's this: was it really God who asked Abraham to sacrifice Isaac? Or was it one of the threshold guardians?

Let's take a deeper dive into that word Heiser maintains is so problematical: 'elohim'.

Of its thousands of appearances in Scripture, 373 of them[7] are the construction, 'ha'elohim'. This means simply '*the* elohim.' It's obviously tempting to think, 'So what?' because translators have entirely disregarded 'ha', *the*, at the beginning. But the question is: why would anyone insert a definite article, a *the*, in the first place? It seems pointless if there is no essential differentiation between 'elohim' and '*the* elohim.'

Often we can gain clues by looking at the time a particular word or phrase is initially introduced. The first time 'ha'elohim' appears is in a snippet about Enoch, the great-grandfather of Noah. The second time it appears involves a repeat of the same wording two verses later. Both instances are about Enoch walking with 'ha'elohim'. Genesis 5:24 BSB says:

> *Enoch walked with God, and then he was no more, because God had taken him away.*

> (*Enoch walked with* ha'elohim; *then he was no more, for* elohim *took him*.)

The principle of looking at the worldview of contemporary readers raises the strong possibility that 'ha'elohim' in this instance actually means *angels*.[8] Not angels as *messengers*, since that specific word 'malak' is not used here, but rather angels in a wider sense as the general class of *heavenly beings*.

According to the Book of 1 Enoch, a collection of stories about the patriarch Enoch that is quoted in the Bible, Enoch was well-acquainted with angels. 1 Enoch was, for some parts of the early Christian world, considered a canonical work—that is, an inspired writing that was to be counted as 'Scripture', Holy Writ. In that book, Enoch was instructed to deliver a judgment to the Watchers, those fallen angels who descended to Mount Hermon and who bound themselves by mutual curses to seek out human women as mates. Enoch conversed with these angels and journeyed in visions and dreams on their behalf, taking a petition to heaven to ask for forgiveness for them where he met with the Lord. Later on, after these events, he embarked on a series of journeys with the angel Uriel through various forbidding realms.

Both God and angels appear prominently in the stories about Enoch. When he is first revealed in 1 Enoch 12, it is mentioned that he was hidden to that point with 'the Watchers and holy ones'. In the book of 2 Enoch, he sat with the Lord and with Gabriel as the days of creation were explained to him, and he was given a prophecy of a future flood that would destroy the earth. He was considered throughout these various texts to be a companion of angels, and back in 1 Enoch he was described as showing to his great-grandson Noah the angels who were preparing the flood.

It would make at least as much sense, given this background, for 'ha'elohim' to mean *the angels* as *God*. And if there is meant to be any distinction between 'ha'elohim' at the beginning of Genesis 5:24 and 'elohim' at the end, then it would be *angels* for 'ha'elohim' and *God* for 'elohim'. In fact, to be consistent with Hebrews 11:5, 'elohim' necessarily has to be God.

The translation that Enoch walked primarily *'with God'* rather than *'with angels'* seems to first emerge in the writings of Ben Sirach in the Book of Ecclesiasticus.[9] It's consequently difficult to be sure which variation, *'with God'* or *'with angels'*, is more accurate because, as we've noted, 'elohim' is a rather ambiguous term denoting *inhabitants of the heavenly realms*.

Still, I believe the weight of evidence is on the side of most readers at the time seeing 'ha'elohim' as meaning *the angel hosts*. By the principle of first mention, this also means we can't discount 'ha'elohim' meaning *angels* in other and later contexts.

Granted, it would require a bit of a rethink about the 'bene ha-elohim', *sons of God*, in Genesis 6:2 and Genesis 6:4, but it doesn't distort our understanding of events to translate the verse,

> *Now the earth was corrupt in God's sight and was full of violence.*
>
> Genesis 6:11 NIV

in this alternate fashion:

> *Now the earth was corrupt because of the angels and was full of violence.*

This is precisely the understanding of ancient readers. For them, the fallen angels were purveyors of forbidden knowledge. This included a range of arts from weaponry to astrology, from cosmetics to divination, from spell-binding to magical medicine. Warfare and all the violence attached to it came through the teaching of the angels—that was the ancient Israelite view. By contrast, the peoples of other nations saw the angel-equivalents, their own demi-gods such as the 'apkallu' of Mesopotamia, as culture heroes who had brought civilisation to mankind. The Israelites, on the other hand, saw the angelic incursion as responsible for the destruction of mankind, both morally and materially. For them, the flood came to preserve the last of humanity from the depredations of the gigantic *nephilim* and their offspring, the 'mighty men of old'.

Most of the 373 uses of 'ha'elohim' refer to the Ark *of God*, another name for the Ark of the Covenant. And of course, it *is* the Ark *of God*. Yet it is also surmounted by two gold cherubim, two angelic throne guardians, and so it isn't unlikely that people thought of it as the 'Ark of the Angels' because those figures topped it. After all, manna was called the *'bread of angels'*.[10]

Now I don't believe it's possible to prove that 'ha'elohim' means *the angels* and not *God*. But what I want to point out is the possibility it means *the angels* cannot be eliminated. It can't be put beyond all contention.

Now, as you've probably guessed, it is 'ha'elohim' who tests Abraham and not 'elohim' or Yahweh. It is unquestionably, indisputably and definitely Yahweh who ends the test, because it specifically says so. But it's twice mentioned previously that 'ha'elohim' tested Abraham.

> *Now it came to pass after these things that* ha'elohim *tested Abraham.*
>
> Genesis 22:1 NKJV

> *Then they came to the place of which* ha'elohim *had told him. And Abraham built an altar there and placed the wood in order; and he bound Isaac his son and laid him on the altar, upon the wood.*
>
> Genesis 22:9 NKJV

This is immediately followed by:

> *And Abraham stretched out his hand and took the knife to slay his son. But the Angel* [malak] *of the Lord* [Yahweh] *called to him from heaven and said, 'Abraham, Abraham!'*
>
> Genesis 22:10–11 NKJV

There's an abrupt change from 'ha'elohim' to Yahweh. Does the sudden intervention of the 'malak Yahweh'— *the messenger of the Lord*—signal that 'ha'elohim' is, in fact, not *God* after all? Is it possible that 'ha'elohim' are *angels*? Could this be a test set by a group of threshold guardians rather than a trial orchestrated by God? After all, that's what threshold guardians do. They test, they tempt, they try.

But God doesn't. James 1:13 NIV tells us:

When tempted, no one should say, 'God is tempting me.' For God cannot be tempted by evil, nor does He tempt anyone.

This might look as if it refers only to *temptation*, but outside the Bible, the Greek word translated *tempt* basically means *test* or *trial*. Certainly God puts people *on* trial (Deuteronomy 4:34), that is, He brings them into judgment; but nowhere does it say He puts us *through* trials. He obviously allows them, since He clearly permitted a cruel, harrowing and terrible test in the life of Abraham. And He also permitted not just one trial but a devastating set of them to occur in Job's life.

We're apt to make pious pronouncements about God teaching us patience or some other virtue. But that's a rationalisation. He simply uses the trials and tests for our benefit, because He is the redeemer of our lives who can take even the very worst that has ever happened to us and turn it around so that it all works together for our good. He loves us inordinately and will reshape the trauma and the terror, if we let Him, for our blessing and favour.

Now personally, I think it was fallen angels who tested Abraham, not God. Ultimately, the reason I do so is because it was fallen angels who also tested Jesus. And just as Jesus was ministered to by holy angels at the end of His tests, so Abraham received the ministrations of an angel who called to him from heaven. There are parallels too close to ignore, particularly since the tests faced by Jesus and Abraham are, in one sense, identical. They are both about destiny: Abraham's about his calling as the father of nations; Jesus' about His calling as the redeemer of nations.

Still, you may be wondering—as I did—why God would allow a cabal of brutal threshold guardians to test Abraham in such a harsh and callous fashion. Why would God allow the spirit of abuse such free rein in Abraham's life?

I think the answer is simple. Abraham had to make a choice where his loyalty lay. He had, after all, been an enabler of his wife's abuse, he had been co-dependent with her—she as the active perpetrator, he as the passive participant—in allowing mistreatment of Hagar to go on for years. He was completely complicit with the spirit of abuse. It was well past time to decide whether he really served Yahweh—who had revealed Himself in a covenantal name exchange as El Shaddai—or whether it was Belial, the abuser, who was the lord and master of his life.

In a very real sense, Abraham brought the test upon himself.

Prayer

It is vitally important to recognise that prayer is about relationship with our heavenly Father through Jesus, who speaks on our behalf as our mediator. None of the prayers in this book are intended to be a formula. They are meant to be guidelines to help you realign yourself with the holy Trinity; they are nothing in or of themselves; they are certainly not 'powerful' or 'effective'—it is only Jesus as our mediator and advocate who can make them so. They are therefore meant as a starting point, to help as a kickstart and give you the mustard seed of faith needed, if you're feeling overwhelmed by new insight. They are not as an end in themselves.

Transformation and healing is only possible as you hold onto the hem of Jesus' prayer shawl and ask Him to intercede before the Father for you.

In the end, it's all about Yeshua, the Messiah!

Abba, Father, Lord of justice and mercy, King of truth and peace, Maker and Creator of all realms and times, thank You for knowing me and loving me.

Thank You that we are saved by Your grace through faith; not through our knowledge of who You are. If I did not have Your favour, then could I even approach Your throne and experience the wonder of You and the sweetness of Your glory? If I needed to know You before I was able to speak to You, I would wander forever in darkness.

Even now, my knowledge of You and of Your Kingship and Your Kingdom is so tiny, so thin, so tenuous. But through Your blessing, I am growing in understanding; through Your empowering strength, I am maturing in faith, in goodness, in knowledge, in self-control, in perseverance, in godliness, in mutual kindness, in devoted love. Thank You for transforming me—even when it's five steps forward and four steps back.

Abba, sometimes my vision of who You really are and what You are really like has been impaired, faulty, just plain wrong. Sometimes I've been disappointed in You because I've misunderstood You. Sometimes I've secretly thought You've been responsible for events that were actually orchestrated by Your enemies. Sometimes I've failed to understand that, just because You've taken responsibility for cleaning up the mess, it doesn't mean You caused it in the first place. Sometimes I just want to blame You because, like children who turn on the parent they know will always love them and not on the parent abusing them, it's safe to accuse You and to project my hatred of others onto You. Sometimes I want You to override the free will of others, ignoring the reality that if You did that then You'd be just like the abuser who controls, coerces and dominates me.

Forgive me for forgetting that and for wanting that; forgive me for believing lies about You, forgive me for hiding blame of You deep in my inmost heart away from my conscious mind. I repent of being double-minded about loving and honouring You.

I ask You to help me know You as You truly are, not a pale shadow of You or a distortion of You, but the real, authentic You in all Your paradox, all the things I'd rather not face, all Your wonder and glory and holy magnificence.

In Jesus' name. Amen.

2

Except God Alone

'Why do you call Me good?' Jesus asked him.
'No one is good except God alone.'

Mark 10:18 GNT

No one is good except God alone.

If we kept this single thought in mind as we look into Scripture, we'd save ourselves from so much misunderstanding. There's a certain flatness about any literal translation of the Bible that used to concern me as I read—because I thought it was a deficiency in me that I so rarely responded with whole-hearted emotion to the text. Now I think the flatness is one of its remarkable strengths. Scripture is not trying to sell us anything. It's not using marketing techniques to guide us to a pre-determined response. It records history, generally without comment, and thus without attempting to manipulate our perception or sway our perspective. It respects our free will and does not try to influence it unduly. With notable exceptions, it is neutral in its presentation, allowing us to make up our own minds about events.

Unfortunately, because we've been taught to read with the hero, rather than with the text, we've tended to think that divine approval rests on the star of whatever passage we're looking at. Sincerity means a lot to us. Nehemiah, for example, is unquestionably a man of integrity. But did he and Ezra do the right thing in forcing the men of Israel to divorce their wives and send them and their children away? This is one case where we actually have God's commentary on their actions. Not, of course, in either the book of Ezra or of Nehemiah, but in the life of Jesus.

When Jesus asked a marginalised, five-times-married woman of Samaria for a drink of water, He was effectively asking her to be the cupbearer of a king. That was precisely Nehemiah's role—so, in this subtle way, by giving the woman an opportunity to be a herald and an ambassador to her town, He re-integrated her into the wider community. He did the opposite of Nehemiah and Ezra.

Additionally, Jesus showed a great deal of honour to Saul, Israel's first king, the traditional 'villain' in the cycle of stories about David. He did this, on His way to raise Lazarus from the dead, by re-tracing the path the bones of Saul and Jonathan took when they were disinterred at David's command and reburied close to Jerusalem. In the process He was undoing the covenant with Sheol that Saul took out the night before he died.

Still, His actions are so unexpected. It's not simply that the King of the Universe has shown such deep humility as to honour a flawed, human king. We don't think of this because, to us, it's unthinkable. Saul, after all, is the bad guy. And David is the good guy. That's our conditioning.

No one is good except God alone.

It needs to be written indelibly on our hearts. There is only one hero in Scripture. Only one. His name is Jesus.

Abraham is the good guy. That's our conditioning too. Many writers have said that Abraham was tested ten times and he passed each and every one of them. There's considerable debate over what exactly the ten tests were, so lists vary. But most contain his encounters with Pharaoh and with Abimelech. Now, I'm not sure how deceiving a monarch—a half-lie about Sarah being his sister and giving the impression she is not his wife—can be considered passing a test, but apparently some people see it that way. It's not as if the deception is without dire consequences—many Egyptians die because of the lie. Frankly I don't believe Abraham passed this test. In fact, I think he was given a second chance at it twenty-five years later. The situation with Abimelech of Gerar is so eerily similar to the events with Pharoah in Egypt two decades before that it cannot be other, in my view, than a further opportunity to pass a failed test.

Yet, Abraham folds and flunks once again. Despite a deepening relationship with El Shaddai through an ongoing series of divine covenants, he still didn't trust God enough to believe in His complete protection. A part of Abraham's heart simply couldn't believe that God would still be his covenant defender in this particular circumstance: when he took his wife to a foreign country. Once again, he instructs Sarah to say she is his sister, a half-truth that conceals as much as it reveals. Because of Abraham and Sarah's duplicity, the women of Gerar were kept from conceiving. The nation itself was in deep peril, as Abimelech pointed out when he finally confronted Abraham.

These stories about tests, of course, raise the question: *who* set them? Was it Yahweh?

Again, it's difficult to tell. In Genesis 20:3, 'elohim' appears to Abimelech in a dream, telling him he's as good as dead for taking Sarah as his wife. This is the wake-up call that shocks Abimelech since he's entirely innocent of wrong-doing, having taken both Sarah and Abraham at their word that they were brother and sister. However, three verses later in Genesis 20:6, still within the same dream sequence, it is 'ha'elohim' who commends Abimelech for his integrity and acknowledges his clear conscience. Later in Genesis 20:17, Abraham prayed to 'ha'elohim' on behalf of Abimelech and his household, and then 'elohim' healed the women of Gerar.

The uncomfortable thought here is that Abraham might have *prayed* to angels. Well, actually more like *intervened* with the angels, *negotiated* with them on Abimelech's behalf. Still, 'pray' is so nuanced to us nowadays with overtones of *worship*, we wouldn't want to think that Abraham, a man who spent seventy-five years in a pagan environment, would waver in his faith, would we? Because those of us brought up in a Christian environment are never complicit with any of the threshold guardians, are we?

Get real.

Our complicity is so deep it's often unspeakable. The more I find false refuges in my own life and I repent of them, the more evident it becomes that there are subtle clusters of unbelief lodged in my heart and carefully hidden from my sight. I vacillate, and I find it difficult to believe that Abraham would not have. In fact, this very story shows his faith as imperfect. It shows his sometimes-suprahuman heroism is marred by the doubts and the common frailty of humanity. Yes, he had deep faith, but it was not unalloyed, it was not unblemished.

Abraham not only faltered in his faith when he went to Gerar and asked Sarah to conceal the fact they were married, he deliberately put the local people in harm's way. He was aware that, back in Egypt two-and-a-half decades previously, the consequences of his deception were the deaths of many people. Yet even knowing that, even knowing that events might repeat themselves, even knowing that there might be citizens of Gerar who would die simply because he didn't trust God enough to tell the full truth, he went ahead with the manipulation anyway.

This is dark, abusive and hard of heart. In many ways, it was important for Abraham to pray—whether it was *asking* or *interceding* or *intervening* or *negotiating*, and also regardless of whether it was with God or with angels—because that action indicates his acknowledgement of responsibility for the tragedy that unfolded. Had Abraham just been allowed to saunter out of Gerar, laden with gifts but without any confession of liability, he would not have been held to account for his abuse, at least at a human level. Nor for his long-standing complicity with the spirit behind it.

No one is good except God alone.

Why do the stories of abuse in Scripture elude us? Why do we paint the perpetrators as champions of faith when their actions are, at times, so unheroic? Why do so many commentators, both Jewish and Christian, say Abraham passed this test when he was totally prepared to sacrifice the lives of the people of Gerar to save his own skin? Is the group mind control, practised by the spirit of abuse, so pervasive that it even influences scholars writing biblical commentary? How often do we ignore the words of Jesus:

No one is good except God alone.

Returning to the question of the identity of 'ha'elohim' throughout the story of Abraham, let's look at his historical setting within the biblical timeline. Just prior to Abraham's family moving out from Ur, we read the account of the Tower of Babel. This places Abraham's life somewhen around the same general time period. It further means that the incident involving Abimelech of Gerar is not too long after God had granted the governance of the nations of the earth to seventy angels, reserving only for Himself the land and people of Israel.

> *God Most High gave land to every nation. He assigned a guardian angel to each of them but the Lord Himself takes care of Israel.*
>
> Deuteronomy 32:8–9 CEV

Now if you check your favourite Bible version, you're more than likely to find there are no angels mentioned in these verses. That's because the Masoretic text, which dates from about a thousand years ago, sanitised the verse and amended it to say that God divided up the world into nations according to *the number of the sons of Israel*. More recent English translations rely on the Dead Sea Scrolls, which are backed up by the Septuagint, both at least a thousand years older than the Masoretic text. Those more ancient versions say, *'the number of the sons of God.'*

Either way, it's seventy. That's the number of Jacob's descendants who went down to Egypt, and so are classed as his 'sons'. And seventy is the number of the principalities set as rulers over the nations. However, with the *'sons of God'*, we are back to the 'bene ha'elohim'. And if we're looking at the timeline of events, the handover of the nations to the guardianship of these angels occurred either not long before Abraham's lifetime or actually within it.

So, in going to Gerar, Abraham was venturing into territory ruled by an angel prince, not by Yahweh. And that angel would have had a vested interest in protecting Abimelech and his household and warning him about the danger he was in. Not only that, it had been such a relatively short time since the angels received their roles as national rulers that they probably hadn't yet undergone the tragic descent into corruption described in Psalm 82. No doubt they were on their way, but it's unlikely to have happened with such rapidity that they were already completely sunk in degeneracy.

So it's quite possible that Abraham, who was used to talking to God and had, in the very recent past, tried to negotiate with Him over the fate of Sodom and Gomorrah, would be prepared to talk to a lesser heavenly being, an angelic principality, and ask it to relent.[11] Furthermore, if an angel with divine authority recognised that Abraham, despite his deception, was still under Yahweh's covering, and yet this angel was also charged with defending the nation under his protection, what were his options? Not many, really.

It should be noted that, in my view, this principality who oversaw Gerar,[12] was not a threshold guardian. It is my understanding, based on experience, that these are not the same. In describing the Armour of God, Paul says:

> *We do not wrestle against flesh and blood, but against* PRINCIPALITIES, *against* POWERS, *against the* THE RULERS OF THE DARKNESS OF THIS AGE.
>
> Ephesians 6:12 NKJV

PRINCIPALITIES ('archons'): angel-princes who govern cities, territories or nations.

POWERS ('exousia'): celestial majesties who, in my experience, watch over frontiers between territories or nations, and are also sentinels over transitions in space, time or state. They are what I call 'threshold guardians'.

RULERS OF THE DARKNESS OF THIS AGE ('kosmokrators'): cosmic rulers or world powers. Their name implies that they may be planetary potentates.

Abraham, I believe, had a threshold guardian on his case at the same time as he was confronting a principality. He had created a terribly fraught situation, in the spiritual realm as well as the earthly.

Now if, as James says, God doesn't test or tempt people, who was doing the testing during the time Abraham and Sarah were in Gerar? I believe it is one or more of the threshold guardians. One of my reasons for thinking so is that Abraham has only very recently participated in three covenants with God, one of which was a threshold covenant. Now, that means he had four covenants with God of various kinds, but it is the last three that are of interest.

Now normally, a threshold guardian will turn up with a temptation at the threshold, but God was visiting Abraham with an angelic escort during the making of this one, so Gerar was obviously a more convenient time to conduct the testing. What does a threshold guardian want? Simple: it wants us to make a *sacrifice*, to worship it, to compromise any covenants we have with Yahweh so that His protection will be withdrawn.

As I've pointed out in previous books, we usually make one of three kinds of sacrifice when we surrender to a threshold guardian:

- we sacrifice someone else or their calling and destiny
- we sacrifice ourselves or our own calling and destiny
- we sacrifice the honour of God and the honour of His name

It's Abraham's willingness to sacrifice the lives of the people of Gerar, in the full knowledge that many Egyptians died in very similar circumstances, that convinces me he was being tested at this point by the spirit of abuse. And because of his willingness, it wasn't the last test he faced of this nature. His failure to trust Yahweh, despite the four covenants, indicates that his commitment to God was far from strong.

Before I give a brief summary of those covenants—BLOOD, NAME, THRESHOLD and SALT—I want to point out that a covenant is contractual, but is so much more as well. When we describe divine covenant basically in terms of promises and obligations, it's like pointing to a duckpond in order to image the sea. Covenant is vastly more than contract; its essential character is *oneness*.

Now there are different onenesses. There's the oneness of family, the oneness of marriage, the oneness of defence. Theologically speaking, over the last century and a half, we've scrunched every kind of covenant down, squeezing all their different aspects in under the umbrella of blood covenant. In phasing the others— name, threshold, salt and peace—out of existence, we failed to understand that our relationship with God is meant to mature over time and move to different levels. A blood covenant brings us into the family of God and makes us His child. But just as not every child becomes a friend of their parents, so not every child of God raises a name covenant and becomes His friend.

In a BLOOD COVENANT with God, all the obligations are His. None are ours. Just as Abraham was asleep when God cut a blood covenant with him, so we are 'asleep', dead in our sins, when He covenants with us to bring us into His family and call us His child.

When He proposes a NAME COVENANT, the obligations become mutual. We're awake now, after all. It's time to move on from childhood and shoulder our responsibilities. When God calls us to be His friend, it's because we've demonstrated loyalty and commitment to Him. This is important for our own safety because friendship changes the dynamic. For the first time, treachery is possible. Enemies don't betray, friends do. And because the obligations are now mutual, betrayal has terrible consequences.

Six days after a name covenant with God, He'll institute a threshold covenant and salt covenant. A THRESHOLD COVENANT—also known as a CORNERSTONE COVENANT—involves hospitality and constitutes an agreement of mutual defence. It's like saying: 'You and I are one when either of us is attacked. I will defend you as if I'm defending myself. I will fight to the death on your behalf.'

A SALT COVENANT simply guarantees the permanency of the other covenants. The COVENANT OF PEACE, which is so rare that—apart from Jesus—only the high priest Phinehas ever seems to have been granted it, comes from a willingness to be one with a curse. Jesus has already fulfilled this on our behalf.

Now because of the theological crushing of all covenants into a singularity—the blood covenant—we entirely miss the importance of faithfulness to God as our response to grace. We are saved by grace through faith but, unless our faith produces faithfulness, we'll be forever on a diet of milk, not meat. We'll be babies, not adults who have demonstrated by a constancy of devotion that we are safely able to be friends with God.

The blood covenant between Abram and God has some decidedly peculiar aspects. It occurred about fourteen years before the name covenant between them, with its name exchange of El Shaddai and Abraham, and its sign of circumcision. The name covenant was quickly followed six days later[13] by a threshold and a salt covenant. This length of time, fourteen years, demonstrates that despite the blip of doubt that resulted in the birth of Ishmael, Abram was still faithful to the blood covenant he had participated in:

> *As the sun was setting, Abram fell into a deep sleep, and suddenly great terror and darkness overwhelmed him.*
>
> *Then the Lord said to Abram, 'Know for certain that your descendants will be strangers in a land that is not their own, and they will be enslaved and mistreated four hundred years. But I will judge the nation they serve as slaves, and afterward they will depart with many possessions. You, however, will go to your fathers in peace and be buried at a ripe old age. In the fourth generation your descendants will return here, for the iniquity of the Amorites is not yet complete.'*
>
> *When the sun had set and darkness had fallen, behold, a smoking firepot and a flaming torch appeared and passed between the halves of the carcasses. On that day the Lord made a covenant with Abram, saying, 'To your descendants I have given this land—from the river of Egypt to the great River Euphrates—the land of the Kenites, Kenizzites, Kadmonites, Hittites, Perizzites, Rephaites, Amorites, Canaanites, Girgashites, and Jebusites.'*
>
> Genesis 15:12-21 BSB

As I've pointed out in the previous book in this series, *Dealing with Belial*, the promise to Abram that his descendants would be slaves, abused and mistreated in a foreign land, is a highly unusual feature for a covenant. In fact, it's right-off-the-charts weird. That Abram didn't protest about it is stranger still.

Abraham tried to negotiate with God on a number of occasions. Once he put in a plea for Ishmael, and on another occasion he seriously bargained with the Lord over the imminent fate of Sodom and Gomorrah. But when it came to his descendants becoming slaves, not a word. Not a peep.

> *Know for certain that your descendants will be strangers in a land that is not their own, and they will be enslaved and mistreated four hundred years.*

I'd like to think it's unnatural, on hearing there's such an ominous judgment hanging over your great-grandchildren, that you don't try to change the outcome. But then I'm reminded Hezekiah did much the same. On being informed his action of showing the Babylonian envoys his entire treasury meant his descendants would wind up eunuchs in the east, he is thankful it won't occur in his own lifetime.

The key words in God's words to Abram are *strangers, enslaved, mistreated*. As soon as God finishes His covenant speech, it becomes entirely evident why this promise was included. An ancient reader or listener on reaching this disturbing decree within the covenantal oath would naturally have wondered what Abram did to deserve this. The answer is immediate. The moment that the covenant scene is over, we are introduced to someone who is *enslaved* and *mistreated* and whose name means *the stranger.* She is Hagar, the servant of Sarai. And her story is like a lingering background perfume all the way through the test that involves Isaac.

It became obvious to Sarai that God's promise to Abram about his multitude of descendants was in jeopardy because she couldn't conceive. So she suggested her husband take Hagar as his second wife. That way, any children would *technically* be Sarai's. Hagar quickly became pregnant and got a lot uppity as a result. Sarai complained to Abram, who wiped his hands of the matter and, instead of protecting Hagar, gave Sarai open season.

Hagar was then so severely abused by Sarai that she fled. Lost on a desert road, she encountered an angel who greeted her by name—a name that Sarai never used. The angel, 'malak Yahweh', *the messenger of God*, told Hagar to return to Sarai, promised her that her descendants would be an uncountable multitude (hmm… sound familiar?) and told her to name her son 'Ishmael'. In response to this marvellous vision, she becomes the first person in all of Scripture to give God a name. She calls Him *'the God who sees me,'* and names the spring of water where she encountered the angel as Beer Lahai-Roi, *Well of the Living One Who Sees Me.*

Fast forward about seventeen years. Sarai has become Sarah, Abram has become Abraham—and they've had a child together: Isaac, *he laughs*. That's the usual translation though, as noted in *Dealing with Belial*, it's actually a name with rich, complex overtones. Its resonances include *lintel, cloud, thin covering, third heaven, glory*.

During a party celebrating the weaning of Isaac, Ishmael laughs at his little brother. Many translations say *mocked*, but that's an interpretation. It may be valid, it may not be. Ishmael's laugh is in fact *exactly* the same as Sarah's laugh when she heard God say she would have a child. It's the same laugh as that encoded in Isaac's name. If Ishmael mocked, then Sarah mocked. If she didn't, then he didn't. It's quite possible that Ishmael was simply playing with Isaac, and they were having fun together. It's natural to laugh when a toddler is being cute. But the laugh reminded Sarah that Ishmael was the firstborn, the inheritor of a double portion of Abraham's wealth. Under the near eastern societal laws of the time pertaining to similar situations, there was only one way she could change that outcome: she would have to release Hagar from slavery and persuade Abraham to divorce her. Then the son could be dispossessed, and both mother and son sent away.

When Sarah demanded the expulsion of Hagar and Ishmael, Abraham was distressed. But God ('elohim') told him to do as Sarah said. Personally, I suspect that was because Sarah's cruelty had reached a critical level. She had engineered the birth of Ishmael, he was technically her son, but she no longer saw him that way. He was a commodity to be thrown away as soon as his usefulness was over.

Sarah hadn't mellowed over the years and become less abusive. She'd experienced a little of Hagar's world when she was in Abimelech's harem in Gerar, but it didn't give her any empathy. She still hadn't used Hagar's name. It's still 'my slave woman', not even 'your other wife'.

When Sarah and Abraham were exiled from Gerar, they were loaded with gifts. When they were exiled from Egypt, they were also loaded with gifts. The merchandise showered on them on each occasion was enough to make them fabulously wealthy. Now I twice used the word 'exiled' for a very good reason. The events in Egypt and Gerar contain echoes of the banishment from Eden.

Pharaoh had piled on the favour for the privilege of acquiring Abram's beautiful 'sister' for the Egyptian court. Doing the honourable thing and paying the family handsomely, he'd loaded Abram up with slaves, sheep, cattle, donkeys and camels, silver and gold. So, he was utterly horrified to finally discern the cause of the plague devastating his country. Sending for Abram, he asked: *'What is this you have done to **me**?'*

His anguished question foreshadows the almost identical cry of Abimelech to Abraham: *'What is this you have done to **us**?'*[14]

'What is this you have done?' God had asked Eve.

That's the only time previously these words have been used.

To justify Abraham's behaviour is to justify abuse. The horror Pharaoh felt about Abram's deception is reflected in his words of dismissal. The last time the Hebrew word for *'Go!'* was used this way was when God cursed the serpent while expelling Adam and Eve from Eden.

I sometimes wonder if, when we identify with particular characters in Scripture, we take on their worst traits as well as their best. I once knew a leader who, every time we caught up with one another, would fill me in on the latest episode in her 'Abrahamic journey'. It was only in the final months of her life that a different light began to be shed on some of those 'Abrahamic' episodes as some of her close associates began to reveal the abusive control she'd exerted over their lives.

No one is good except God alone.

We're not called to follow Abraham. We're called to follow Jesus.

Abraham and Sarah were exiled from Egypt but they were treated with exceptional honour. Abimelech sent them away but said, 'Settle where you like.' They'd received an overflow of blessing while twice being cast out, but couldn't pass it on. Of all those herds of sheep, cattle, donkeys and camels bestowed on Abraham and

Sarah in Egypt and Gerar, they apparently couldn't spare one for Hagar and Ishmael. They gave them no more food and water than what they could carry.

God may have told Abraham to agree with Sarah in sending Hagar and Ishmael away but He didn't say to treat them heartlessly. An overnight guest is likely to have received more valuable gifts than the bags of food and skins of water Hagar was given for her twenty, perhaps thirty, years of service. I honestly have to suspect Sarah didn't want them to survive. She apparently wanted them dead.

I further have to suspect that's why God instructed Abraham to send them away. Their lives were in danger if they stayed. They were a threat to Sarah's ambitions for her son.

Gillian Bradshaw in her novel, *The Bearkeeper's Daughter*, makes the acute observation, 'A man, or a woman, may be indifferent to money and honest with authority, but because he wishes to establish his children in riches and power, he may be willing to sell justice, corrupt, lie, scheme, even murder and think he's doing nothing wrong, because he does it for his children. Dynastic ambition.'

I know people who lost the integrity it had taken a lifetime to build, cheating and stealing to establish their children in business. It was unthinkable for them to practise dishonesty to advantage themselves, but for their children, they sold their soul.

Sarah had invested the better part of a century in desperate yearning for the birth of Isaac. She knew God's promises and she wanted them to apply to the son of her own flesh, not the son by a technicality of law. Dynastic ambition? Absolutely. It ate her up.

Through all these episodes, Abraham is complicit with the spirit of abuse operating through Sarah. It comes to function through him in Gerar—because there he unquestionably knew, from previous experience, that he was putting lives at risk through his duplicity.

Now recall that this is the time period in which God has not long previously handed over government of the nations to the seventy principalities. He's reserved Israel to Himself but it's still in the process of being established. He's chosen Abraham to be the father of a nation through whom the entire world will be blessed but, at this point, all of His promises hang on the existence of Isaac. Remove Isaac, and God's plan for redemption through that covenantal line goes up in smoke.

So, because the spirit of abuse has massive inroads into Abraham's life, it can easily be behind any plot to get rid of Isaac. And because one of this spirit's most common and diabolic tactics is to get us to resource the war against ourselves, it would naturally want to influence Abraham to kill his own son and destroy his own destiny. That's the modus operandi of the spirit of abuse: mind control that causes us to sabotage ourselves and yet believe we are acting in God's will.

Is 'ha'elohim' *God* or is it *the angels* in the story of the binding of Isaac?

Abraham has so much complicity with the spirit of abuse over so many decades, I can see why it would have the legal right to test him and thereby hope to achieve its nefarious goal. Belial, after all, was the prime mover in the previous plot to destroy God's plans for humanity's redemption—the descent of the 'sons of God' to mate with beautiful women and create violence in the earth. Belial doesn't want God to establish a human family and choose new 'sons of God'. And this was its next big chance to spoil God's design for salvation.

Just below the surface of the story of Isaac and Abraham's journey to Mount Moriah is a sub-strata of parallels with Hagar's flight from abuse. In fact, the story suspiciously ends up at the very same spring of water, Beer Lahai-Roi, suggesting that we are meant to see the connection between the two. Because we've strained to fit the binding of Isaac into a theological schema where God is good but the test was at God's instigation, we've missed the obvious connection: actually, this is about Abraham's allegiance with the spirit of abuse.

Part of his heart was fully devoted to God and chose to believe Him utterly—his faith was counted as righteousness. But another part of his heart was off, dallying with the leader of the rebel Watchers. He'd been a complacent onlooker when it came to violence. He'd then become a passive perpetrator of abuse through allowing the consequences of his deceptions to go unchecked: plague in Egypt, infertility in Gerar. Granted that he didn't know when he went to Egypt what the outcome of his manipulation of truth would be, but that same ignorance did not apply when he travelled to Gerar.

Now, assuming that 'ha'elohim' who ask for the sacrifice of Isaac are indeed *the angels* and not God, why would God allow such a test to go ahead? It actually doesn't solve any issues around the goodness and lovingkindness of God to suggest that He permitted angels to do this but was not directly involved Himself. Why didn't He speak up sooner? Why did He leave it until the very last moment to intervene?

Because He does indeed intervene. The Angel of the Lord, the 'malak Yahweh', *the messenger of God*, appears and calls Abraham's name from heaven. Angels have been a very prominent feature throughout Abraham's story—so prominent they are almost routine. There have been the angels who were God's escorts on His visit to the tents of Abraham and who then went on to rescue Lot from the destruction of Sodom. There was the angel ('malak elohim') who directed Hagar's attention to a well when she and Ishmael were lost in the desert of Beersheba and dying of thirst after being cast out of the tents of Abraham. But the last time the specific words 'malak Yahweh' were used was before Ishmael was born and Hagar was fleeing abuse.

The 'malak Yahweh' addresses people by name. He called to Abraham on Mount Moriah by name. He also called to Hagar at Beer Lahai-Roi by name. This is notable because neither Abraham nor Sarah ever did. Hagar was so touched by the angel's intervention she named God *'the Living One who sees me'.* Abraham was so touched by the angel's intervention that he called God, 'Yahweh Yireh', *the God who sees*. Often 'yireh' is translated *provide* but its etymological root is *see*.

We not only have the 'malak Yahweh' calling by name in both instances, we find that both Hagar and Abraham respond in similar ways. Abraham, in fact, basically confirmed the name Hagar had given to God. Here, I believe, we witness Abraham awakening to his own complicity when Yahweh opens his eyes.

Such are the deep parallels between the flight of Hagar and the binding of Isaac. The final link occurs much later in the narrative. After Abraham is directed to sacrifice a ram caught in the thicket, Isaac is not heard of again for some chapters. Abraham came down the mountain and returned to his servants but there is no mention of Isaac's presence. There's no comment about him right through the retelling of the death of Sarah. A first-time reader is left in suspense—is Isaac alive or not?

We can finally presume he is indeed in the land of the living, because Abraham sends his servant back to Aram to get a bride for him. Yet Isaac himself is still mysteriously absent. When he does finally reappear, we're told:

> *Now Isaac had come from Beer Lahai-Roi, for he was living in the Negev.*
>
> Genesis 24:62 NIV

Isaac had gone to the very place which Hagar had named after meeting the Angel of the Lord. Did Isaac flee from his father at Moriah, just as Hagar had once fled from his mother? Eventually we discover that, when Isaac and Ishmael are together at the tomb of Sarah to bury Abraham, that a reconciliation had occurred between the half-brothers. The text subtly hints that Isaac was the facilitator and that, perhaps, he went straight from Mount Moriah to Beer Lahai-Roi in order to find Ishmael and Hagar. He'd just experienced a deep trauma. He needed to be able to process the feelings associated with it and come to terms with the shock, so it would be logical for him to seek support from those who were resilient in the face of abuse—and that certainly wasn't either of his parents.

Had he not worked through what happened to reach forgiveness, spiritual abuse would have rocketed down the generations from that point. This is true, regardless of whether 'ha'elohim' is *the angels* or *the Lord*.

As you've no doubt realised, I personally think the Akedah, *the binding of Isaac*, was at the instigation of the threshold guardians, led by Belial. I believe there's more than a fair chance that the spirit of abuse was the one behind the terrible test inflicted on Abraham. Because Belial has been erased from most translations or else degenerated into the 'personification' of *worthlessness*—

an attribute, not an entity—then it's necessary to render 'ha'elohim' as *God*, not because it necessarily is God but simply because there's no other choice.

We can say for sure, however, that Yahweh intervened—and not only intervened, He was able to use this test for a great good. It was to point out to all future generations that idol worship involving child sacrifice might be common out among the nations but it was not to be practised amongst the people who descended from Abraham.

God hates abuse. In the very first divine covenant between Himself and Abraham, God spelled out the generational reaping that would occur for tolerating and, by default, enabling it. Even with that knowledge, Abraham did not attempt to minimise the future reaping by repenting. Continuing his complicity, he eventually became an abuser himself.

How often is that the story today, particularly in our churches, schools, governmental bodies. When we tolerate abuse, sooner or later we become inflictors of it. As we view the story of Abraham, we see the mercy of God written large. He gave Abraham time to change. But time eventually came against him.

Prayer

Heavenly Father, I confess: *no one is good except You alone.*

Lord Jesus Christ, I confess: *no one is good except You alone.*

Holy Spirit, I confess: *no one is good except You alone.*

Blessed Trinity, Father, Son and Holy Spirit, I confess: *no one is good except You alone.*

Father, when I tempted to put myself on a pedestal, remind me: *no one is good except You alone.* When I'm tempted to put one of my parents on a pedestal, remind me: *no one is good except You alone.* When I'm tempted to put one of my children on a pedestal, remind me: *no one is good except You alone.* When I'm tempted to put my love on a pedestal, remind me: *no one is good except You alone.* When I'm tempted to put my boss on a pedestal, remind me: *no one is good except You alone.* When I'm tempted to put a celebrity on a pedestal, remind me: *no one is good except You alone.* When I'm tempted to put a worship leader on a pedestal, remind me: *no one is good except You alone.* When I'm tempted to put anyone I admire—president, politician, pastor, public figure—on a pedestal, remind me: *no one is good except You alone.* When I'm tempted to put any of the heroes of Scripture on a pedestal, remind me: *no one is good except You alone.*

Remind me, Lord, that people are complex mixtures of good and bad. Remind me, Lord, that faith makes a person righteous in Your sight but it doesn't make them good. Remind me, Lord, that miracles and healings done in Your name are gifts of Your grace but no indicators of the goodness of a person, or even if they know You.

Remind me, Lord, that I should never offer to anyone the unreserved trust and unquestioning loyalty due only to You. Lord, forgive me for doing that. Forgive me for the times I've honoured others more than You, for the times I've avoided conflict rather than confront others with truth and grace, for the times I've sided with a person knowing only one side of a story and failing to honour Your requirement of the need for two or three witnesses, for my hypocrisy in absolving leaders of behaviour I won't tolerate in others, for my failure to hold leaders to a higher standard of conduct, for idolising them and then on discovering their flaws being disillusioned in them, for believing I am worthless, for marginalising myself because I expected to be excluded, for deciding I am unfixable, for choosing to think God will heal others but not me because I'm not good enough or I'm too bad to redeem.

Lord, in all the tangled ways my mind is confused about good and bad, help! I have not honoured You as I should, nor praised, nor worshipped, nor glorified You as I should. Help!

Father, I repent of looking to others as my role models of faith, and not to Jesus. I repent of looking to others as my role models of goodness, and not to Jesus. I ask Jesus through the power of His Cross to empower my repentance and to mature in me the Fruit of goodness, kindness and faithfulness.

> In His good and holy name. Amen.

3

Turn Back Time

Know for certain that your descendants will be strangers in a land that is not their own, and they will be enslaved and mistreated four hundred years. But I will judge the nation they serve as slaves, and afterward they will depart with many possessions.

Genesis 15:13–14 BSB

So said Yahweh during the raising of his first covenant with Abram.

The covenant did not negate the sowing-and-reaping principle. Nor does the Blood of the Cross negate the sowing-and-reaping principle. That's despite the oft-repeated protest, 'It's all done at the Cross.' If that were the case, then Paul would not have said to believers:

Do not be deceived; God is not mocked, for you reap whatever you sow.

Galatians 6:7 NRS

This is not to say that the Blood is ineffective, but that it must be *applied* through repentance and forgiveness. There's nothing set to automatic in our relationship with God. Relationships don't operate by default settings, they function differently for each individual through time spent in intimate companionship.

Abraham and Sarah sowed abuse and mistreatment with Hagar, *the stranger*, their Egyptian slave. They or their descendants were due to reap abuse and mistreatment, slavery and indifference, as strangers in Egypt. And that's exactly what comes to pass, as God's decree is fulfilled. It might seem like a punishment, magnified beyond all reason, but it's simply an outworking of one of the immutable building blocks of creation, a law coded into the very fabric of the universe itself.

The sowing-and-reaping principle is a combination of the action-reaction law of physics and the multiplication aspect of agriculture. It's not simply that what goes around comes around, it's that seeds must multiply or we'd always be eating down a dwindling stock of grain. This multiplication principle was obviously designed to be a blessing to mankind so that the world could build itself up in the Fruit of love, joy, peace, patience, kindness, goodness, faithfulness, gentleness and self-control. But, with the Fall, the multiplication principle brings in increased levels of every kind of sin.

The more time it takes for abuse to be dealt with, the more it multiplies. Time, as noted in the previous book in this series, *Dealing with Belial,* is a significant face of the spirit of abuse. This alter-ego of Belial is Kronos, and it is an abuser who consumes the past. It also wants to devour our future by ensuring that the past has never truly passed (and yes, that's meant to be a pun) but intrudes so deeply on the present that it is eaten up by pain.

As an abuser, the spirit of Time is against us, when God actually designed it to be for us. He created days and nights, months and seasons, to be a blessing for us. I often look out my back door to glimpse the red wonder of the western sky at sunset. That's the official start of the day as recorded in Scripture:

> *And there was evening and there was morning, the first day.*
>
> Genesis 1:5 NRS

I marvel at how God brushes the sky in shades of red at sundown and dawn. These, in ancient times, were looked on as the gates of Day. And, just as a doorway would be painted with the blood of a lamb or a calf to welcome a guest, so they are daubed in red as God's invitation to us to be His guest in the coming hours.

Because of their blood-red hue, they are also a reminder of God's covenant with the day and the night.[15]

When God deals with the spirit of abuse, He rolls back Time. He redeems time, He gives us time as a gift of grace, He makes time work in our favour, not in opposition to us. In *Dealing with Belial*, I looked at two episodes in the history of Israel where that happened.

Here's a brief recap on those astonishing events and how the first occasion inspired the second.

The Israelites had conquered the cities of Jericho and Ai, and had then obeyed the instructions of Moses to go to Shechem and reaffirm the covenant with God. While they were there, some envoys arrived in threadbare garments and worn sandals, claiming that they'd heard of the great miracles God had performed on behalf of the people of Israel. They had journeyed, so they said, from a far country to make a covenant with God's chosen people. In fact, the Gibeonites were close neighbours and, as Amorites, God had given an instruction to wipe them out.

Joshua and the Israelite leadership were suspicious about the story offered by the Gibeonite ambassadors but not suspicious enough to inquire of God. Perhaps, since this ultimately turned out to be an episode involving the spirit of abuse, there was some group mind control operating. A few days after making a covenant with the Gibeonites, Joshua discovered the deception. As it turns out, the covenant must have been a threshold one—incorporating mutual defence—because the Gibeonites soon called on their covenant allies to come to their aid.

Now at the point of discovery, the Israelites were in a double-bind. They'd been snared in a conspiracy. A league of four cities in the Gibeonite confederacy had devised a plan to maximise the chances of their own survival in the coming war. But the Israelites were trapped in a spiritual dilemma. Whatever they did, they would be going against

God. If they didn't get raze the Gibeonite cities, then they would disobey God's instructions to remove the people of the land. On the other hand, if they broke the covenant they'd just cut, that would be heinous since, as image-bearers of God, one of the most significant ways we can carry His name is by loyally upholding any covenants we have taken out. He is a covenant-keeping God. That is His essential nature.

The Israelites chose to believe that covenant-keeping was the higher law. So, when the Gibeonite cities were attacked by five kings who took exception to the alliance they'd made, the Israelites responded to the call for help as covenantal obligation required. At this point, when the Israelites armies undertook an all-night march to defend the Gibeonites and, in addition, fight on grounds not of their own choosing, they were—in a very real sense—directly opposing the spirit of abuse. Not only is it a spirit of armies as well as abuse, one of its primary tactics is to get us to resource the war against ourselves.

Now as Joshua was leading the forces of Israel against the five kings, he realised there was one thing he lacked towards complete victory. Time. He needed more time.

Everything else was in place: God had covered the Israelite army, both above and below. A cloud of His protection shot down hailstones—or meteorites—pulverising the five Amorite armies. Beneath their feet was an ancient cornerstone, not of the Amorites, but of the Hebrews. In fact, it was placed there by a member of Joshua's own tribe, so if anyone had a right to invoke any covenantal defence associated with it, he certainly did. As the seventh army on the field that day—the hosts of heaven—came to the aid of the Israelites, Joshua was on the Ascent of Beth Horon, a narrow path between the twin cities of Upper Beth Horon and Lower Beth Horon. This town-planning design imaged a covenant in the landscape. The settlements had been built by Sheerah, the daughter of Ephraim, the son of Joseph and adopted son of Jacob, and were the first cities in the land promised to Abraham to be constructed by one of his descendants. They therefore had the status of a national 'cornerstone'.

It was an ideal situation: cornerstone below, covering cloud above, heavenly hosts assisting. Just one problem: not enough time. So Joshua asked for it. He asked God to show Himself strong as Lord of Time, so that the spirit of abuse, the spirit of armies and the spirit of Time—all three faces—could be comprehensively defeated. Joshua called on God to combat Kronos.

> *On the day that the Lord gave the men of Israel victory over the Amorites, Joshua spoke to the Lord. In the presence of the Israelites he said,*
>
> *'Sun, stand still over Gibeon;*
> *Moon, stop over Aijalon Valley.'*
>
> *The sun stood still and the moon did not move until the nation had conquered its enemies. This is written in The Book of Jashar. The sun stood still in the middle of the sky and did not go down*

for a whole day. Never before, and never since, has there been a day like it, when the Lord obeyed a human being. The Lord fought on Israel's side!

Joshua 10:12–14 GNT

Now, when this was written, there'd never been another day like it. Yet, at a later date, Scripture records Isaiah's prophecy of a further time-altering event.

His words encourage me to believe God will turn back time for us. On behalf of our nation, not for personal advancement.

In Isaiah's day, the people of Jerusalem were faced with terror on every side. The Assyrians had swept across the face of the known world, slaughtering and enslaving as they went, while their kings bragged about the ferocious cruelty they inflicted. Notorious for their vicious torture of rebel officials in dissident kingdoms, the mere thought of their advance was enough to pay them off. King Hezekiah tried this, emptying both the palace and the Temple treasuries of silver and stripping the gold off the doors of the Temple.[16] However, the Assyrians prepared to besiege Jerusalem.

It was an utterly chilling prospect for the leaders. They had no faith in God to save them, so in desperation they turned to the occult. To save themselves from a horrifying death, they made a covenant with the spirit of Death. Like the Gibeonites allying themselves with their enemies, the Israelites, in order to maximise their chances of survival in any coming conflict, the leaders of Jerusalem allied themselves with the most potent enemy of all—Death. It's totally perverted thinking to believe that Death will honour an agreement to save you from itself, but the leaders were no doubt crazy with fear.

But that agreement wasn't enough. As backup, to cover themselves with even more spiritual protection, the leaders also covenanted with Sheol—hell—calling up spirits of the warrior dead to come and battle on their behalf. Such treaties with the underworld and the grave, Isaiah points out, are simply false refuges against the overwhelming might that's camped down in the next valley.

> *Therefore hear the word of the Lord, you scoffers who rule this people in Jerusalem. You boast, 'We have entered into a covenant with Death, with the realm of the dead we have made an agreement. When an overwhelming scourge sweeps by, it cannot touch us, for we have made a lie our refuge and falsehood our hiding place.'*
>
> Isaiah 28:14–15 NIV

But, if you stop mocking and repent, Isaiah points out, God will break through with a miracle the likes of which has not been seen since the days when David defeated the Philistines at Mount Perazim and, before that, when Joshua defeated the Amorites at Gibeon. Yes, more than repentance is needed, Isaiah goes on to say, but the extras will be provided by God Himself. One of those extras, as he points out in the very next verse, is a 'cornerstone'.

So this is what the Sovereign Lord says:

'See, I lay a stone in Zion, a tested stone, a precious cornerstone for a sure foundation; the one who relies on it will never be stricken with panic. I will make justice the measuring line and righteousness the plumb line; hail will sweep away your refuge, the lie, and water will overflow your hiding place. Your covenant with Death will be annulled; your agreement with the realm of the dead will not stand.'

Isaiah 28:16-18 NIV

Now, we know—with the benefit of hindsight—that the cornerstone here is Jesus. Both Peter and Paul said so. But did Isaiah know that? Did the leaders in Jerusalem know that? Of course not! Did they have to wait centuries for Jesus to arrive before they could be saved from the Assyrian invasion? No.

We know that God's intervention was, exactly as Isaiah promised, incredible beyond belief. Here's the promise:

The Lord will rise up as He did at Mount Perazim, He will rouse Himself as in the Valley of Gibeon— to do His work, His strange work, and perform His task, His alien task.

Isaiah 28:21 NIV

What historical events was Isaiah referring to here? He's highlighted two completely different battles, in two completely different eras, but with one thing in common. Victory became assured at the same place. We have very few details about the conflict at Mount Perazim, but the outline of the battle has been reconstructed.[17] Philistine troops had marched up against Jerusalem from a garrison they'd established at Bethlehem. They had come from the south through the Valley of Rephaim, a place named for ghosts and giants and the warrior dead. However the Lord caused a breakthrough (hence the name 'Perazim') against their battalions by sending what seems to have been a wall of water against them as they neared the city. Those who survived the onslaught were pursued by David's forces who were able to drive them north by northwest where their final defeat was secured on the Ascent of Beth Horon.

The second reference—to the Valley of Gibeon—alludes to the story of Joshua who, fighting five armies on the Ascent of Beth Horon about half a millennia before David's battle, asked for the sun to stand still over Gibeon.

The common factor in both these stunning miraculous events—first, a wall of water out of nowhere, reminding us of the wall of water that smashed Pharaoh's armies, and second, time standing still—is the Ascent of Beth Horon. And *both* these events, not just one of them, are also about *time*. I'll come back to the reasons why later.

What Isaiah is saying in chapter 28 is that, with the right Cornerstone—one like the cornerstone built into the landscape at Beth Horon—it's possible to ask God to show Himself strong against the spirit of Time itself and to actually receive from Him the gift of time redeemed or time rolled back. All through the poem encompassing this chapter and beyond are allusions, hidden in Hebrew, to the name Sheerah, the woman who built Beth Horon. All through it too are allusions to abuse, mockery, injustice, armies, violence, reliance on the occult instead of loyalty to God.

Isaiah's prophecy is mind-blowing. Who could believe that, by returning to God and accepting the right Cornerstone and the right Cloud covering, the Lord would respond by not only showing up as the commander of the hosts of heaven to take out the enemy but also by stopping Time?

Actually the Lord went one better than stopping Time. He turned it back.

During the Assyrian siege, Hezekiah was extremely ill. He was so far gone that he was actually at death's door. The Assyrian commander, the Rabshakeh, demanded to see him but met instead with the king's officials by *'the conduit of the upper pool, which is on the road of the fuller's field.'*[18] Curiously, this is exactly the location where, a generation earlier, Isaiah had delivered the prophecy of Immanuel to Hezekiah's father, Ahaz.

Hezekiah received the Rabshakeh's threat from his officials, took it, and laid it out before the Lord in the Temple. This was a critical moment—the king roused himself from his deathbed to turn to God. Isaiah went to him—just as once he'd gone to meet Hezekiah's father, Ahaz, up by the conduit on the road to the fuller's field—with a similar request. He asked Hezekiah to choose what sign he'd prefer from God to show that all would be well—both in the king and in the kingdom.

> *Isaiah said, 'This shall be the sign to you from the Lord, that the Lord will do the thing that He has promised: shall the shadow go forward ten steps, or go back ten steps?'*
>
> *And Hezekiah answered, 'It is an easy thing for the shadow to lengthen ten steps. Rather let the shadow go back ten steps.'*
>
> *And Isaiah the prophet called to the Lord, and He brought the shadow back ten steps, by which it had gone down on the steps of Ahaz.*
>
> 2 Kings 20:9–11 ESV

The steps of Ahaz apparently worked as a sundial. And the shadow went backwards. God showed Himself as Lord of Time.

But there was more. To complete the fulfilment of Isaiah's prophecy that the Lord would fight on behalf of His people as He did at Perazim and Gibeon:

> *That night the angel of the Lord went out and struck down 185,000 in the camp of the Assyrians. And when people arose early in the morning, behold, these were all dead bodies.*
>
> 2 Kings 19:35 ESV

No wonder Isaiah was so revered as a prophet. What he'd promised was a fairytale ending to a terrifying political impasse, and that's what God delivered. Just as Joshua called on the Lord to stop Time, so Isaiah called on Him to roll it back.

Whatever happened that night—and it's not clear from the text itself—God had come as *'a man of war'*.[19] Some commentators think a mice-borne plague took out the Assyrians.[20] However I'm inclined to believe, based solely on Isaiah's prophecy, it was a similar event to the meteorological bombardment that assisted Joshua against the Amorites. That means it was either a salvo of giant hailstones or of meteorites, and it also presupposes a Cloud covering, since hail implies a raincloud and meteorites imply an ionisation cloud.

The Cloud is always there. As I've pointed out in *Dealing with Belial*, it's critical for us to have the Glory Cloud of God covering us when confronting the spirit of abuse.

The Cloud was there for Joshua. It had to have been there for David also during the Philistine offensive at Mount Perazim. On the coast, a tsunami of water may thunder in from the sea, but Jerusalem is too far inland. The deluge had to have come from cloud covering.

Now remember I said that the wall of water was really about Time? The torrent hurtling down at the Philistines was both a symbol and a reminder of God's earlier victory over the armies of Pharaoh. The fleeing Israelites had walked between walls of water before the parted sea had rolled back into place and drowned the Egyptian armies.

> *The people of Israel went into the midst of the sea on dry ground, the waters being a wall to them on their right hand and on their left. The Egyptians pursued and went in after them into the midst of the sea, all Pharaoh's horses, his chariots, and his horsemen. And in the morning watch the Lord in the pillar of fire and of cloud looked down...*
>
> Exodus 14:22–24 ESV

Note in passing that here, once again, is the Cloud.

Now the word for *sea* in this passage is 'yam' sounds very similar to 'yom', *day*,[21] which in most languages is of course related to *light*. Yet the mysterious relationship between *day* and *sea* lingers even in English within the realm of physics. Light is defined by the electromagnetic spectrum and, within the science of electromagnetism, there is constant mention of streams, currents, flows and waves. Words to do with the *sea*.

But then *day* and night are to do with the passage of time. As the tides of the *sea* also show the passage of time in another way. As the phases of the *moon* show it in yet another way. As the *sun* in its seasonal movements shows it in still another way.

Day and sea, moon and sun, seasons and the weather associated with them are all connected with time. Because of this interconnection, when God pulled back the waters of the Red Sea through the power of His breath, He was also drawing up time. He was showing His power as Lord of wind and waves, and also showing Himself strong as Lord of time. He was further showing Himself pre-eminent over Kronos, the spirit of abuse; over Leviathan, the spirit of retaliation; over Rachab, the spirit of wasting.[22]

> *You divided the sea by Your strength; You broke the heads of the sea serpents in the waters. You broke the heads of Leviathan in pieces, and gave him as food to the people inhabiting the wilderness.*
>
> Psalm 74:13–14 NASB
>
> *You rule over the surging sea; when its waves mount up, You still them. You crushed Rahab[23] like one of the slain; with Your strong arm You scattered Your enemies.*
>
> Psalm 89:9–10 NIV

All these threshold guardians were shown up as powerless in the mighty Presence of God.

Having said that there's always the Cloud, there's nothing mentioned overhead in the story of the rolling back of the waters of the Jordan. But perhaps there didn't need to be a protective covering on that occasion—there were, after all, no pursuing armies or fleeing ones either. Joshua and the people of Israel were right on the threshold of the Promised Land. After forty years of wandering the wilderness, only the River Jordan stood between them and their goal.

> *Now the Jordan is at flood stage all during harvest. Yet as soon as the priests who carried the ark reached the Jordan and their feet touched the water's edge, the water from upstream stopped flowing. It piled up in a heap a great distance away, at a town called Adam in the vicinity of Zarethan, while the water flowing down to the Sea of the Arabah (that is, the Dead Sea) was completely cut off. So the people crossed over opposite Jericho. The priests who carried the ark of the covenant of the Lord stopped in the middle of the Jordan and stood on dry ground, while all Israel passed by until the whole nation had completed the crossing on dry ground.*
>
> Joshua 3:15–17 NIV

What a wondrous image. The Jordan piled up in a heap at Adam, the waters rose into a wall, reminding a new generation of the experiences of their parents forty years previously. And if that miraculous event of passing dry-shod through the Sea was a symbol of Time being rolled back, then this too was indicative of a reset of Time.[24]

The river Jordan, along with the flow of Time, rolled back to 'Adam'. It was as if God wanted to indicate a reset of time back to the days of Adam, as if He were saying, 'I am returning you to the Garden.' The land of milk and honey, the land promised to Abraham, was an inheritance of such fertility and fecundity that a single bunch of grapes needed to be carried on a pole between two strong men. It was indeed another chance to begin again.

That image of returning to the Garden of Eden turns up a millennium and a half later in the same general location. Jesus was travelling through Jericho when He stopped under a sycamore, a variety of fig tree. There He spoke to the tax-collector Zacchaeus, who was up the tree, watching out for Him. Jesus, always on the look-out to heal history, knew an ideal opportunity when He saw it.

There is one other time that Scripture mentions someone in a tree, watching out for the coming of God. That person was Adam, but he was keeping an eye out because he was hiding. Most translations say that Adam and Eve hid amongst the 'trees of the garden', but it's more accurate to say they hid 'in the tree'.[25] They clearly climbed it and, because they'd made themselves fig-leaf coverings, it's likely to have been a fig tree. Just like the tree Zacchaeus climbed. To complete the parallel, both Adam and Zacchaeus mean *man*.

Yet the story of Zacchaeus is about a new beginning. And this is what God promises us as He deals with the spirit of abuse for us: He pledges a fresh start, the restoration of inheritance, the redemption of time. That is such a precious aspect of His covenantal defence of us. Yes, He expects obedience. Yet He knows we'll fail. So He wants us to keep short accounts when He points out our disobedience. In short, He wants us to show ourselves committed to Him. He wants us to *repent* of our sins and turn back to Him.

Repentance.

One insidious tactic of the spirit of abuse is to 'deconstruct' words, to switch around commonly accepted meanings so they are back-to-front. An abuser facilitates deception by using words in a redefined way, knowing that listeners are completely unaware of the redefinition.

It's a great shock to find that a word like 'repentance' is no longer understood as it has been for over two millennia but, in truth, we shouldn't be surprised. The last thing Belial-Kronos wants for us is to find help from God, so it has to target our understanding of how to receive it. But if you want God to turn back Time for your nation, first you have to turn back to Him.

As more and more people in the last century began to understand repentance as a gift of grace and apply its life-transforming power, it was important from the standpoint of Belial-Kronos that it be stripped of its ancient meaning and turned against itself. And once we humans have taken on board a perverted understanding of the term, we're simply going to be undermining ourselves every time we engage with our faulty so-called 'repentance'.

Here are some strange modern misunderstandings or evasions of genuine biblical repentance. The list is hardly comprehensive because more mutations of meaning keep popping up all the time.

- ✘ Repentance is unnecessary in a post-resurrection era.
- ✘ Repentance is unnecessary if you've confessed.
- ✘ Repentance is agreeing swiftly and humbly with the Accuser.
- ✘ Repentance is a 'change of mind', not a 'change of behaviour'.
- ✘ Repentance is a misunderstanding of authority; it's better to 'decree and declare'.

Let's look at each of these in a little more detail.

- ✘ *Repentance is unnecessary in a post-resurrection era.*

It must be time for a reminder.

No one is good except God alone.

Paul is not the hero of the New Testament. This might be self-evident to some of us, but not to everyone. Whenever I'm editing and I come across an effusive, extravagant statement about Paul that seems to accord him an elevated, almost demi-god status not unlike the rank the people of Lystra offered him,[26] I tone it back. I'm not kidding about the 'suprahuman divinity' aspect—and I'm not the only one who has noticed it. I've met some pastors who quietly struggle with the tendency of their colleagues to idolise Paul and to exalt his writings not just over those of every other apostle who penned an epistle, but also over the words of Jesus.

It takes a while to discover the thinking behind this disquieting phenomenon. It's simply that Jesus generally spoke *before* the resurrection and Paul wrote *after it,* so, in this worldview, Jesus' words don't necessarily apply. If Paul's comments appear to contradict what Jesus said, then Paul's words are given precedence. It's the Old vs New Testament dichotomy taken to a whole new level.

Now Paul, so I've been told personally, never mentioned confession of sins. So, according to this theological stance, it should be clear to everyone that, after we've made the initial decision to follow Christ and our sins are all cancelled at the cross, there is no further need for confession of sins or for turning away from them in repentance. Because 'it's all done at the Cross' and we live in a post-resurrection world, there is not only no need for it, it's actually a distortion of the gospel to suggest we should 'confess and repent'.

I wonder how a bride would feel if, on her wedding day, the groom said to her, 'I'm sorry for all the ways I've acted in the past that might ever affect our marriage.

Please forgive me. Oh, by the way, this is the last apology you can ever expect from me.' And I wonder how she'd feel, as time went by, when her husband was less than loving but claimed he never had to say sorry because he'd offered a once-for-all apology back at the wedding.

To claim that repentance is about 'The Law' when it's actually about restoration of relationship is a fatally flawed misunderstanding of its nature. Actually, that's a generous assessment on my part. Let me reframe and rephrase. To claim that repentance is about 'The Law' is to invent a theological excuse for wilful arrogance that refuses to admit to wrongdoing.

Because while Paul might not mention confession of sins, John does in his first epistle and so does James. Moreover, Paul mentions repentance which presupposes confession. And then there's Jesus who, in the vision of John in Revelation says to the *believers*—not unbelievers—at Ephesus:

> *Repent and do the things you did at first.*
> Revelation 2:5 NIV

The belief that you only need to repent once in life is an excuse that is little more than a poor justification for pride.

✘ *Repentance is unnecessary if you've confessed.*

Maarit Harden made me aware of this novel way of evading repentance. She'd encountered it repeatedly in counselling, and recognised a false refuge. People who feel guilty about a particular vice they've indulged in, but don't want to give it up, console themselves with the belief that confessing to God is enough to wipe away the penalty. They confess repeatedly—meaning that they've acknowledged to God that they've sinned—but they choose not to turn from the habit. They don't hate it, they love it—and they love it more than they love God. Their consciences are awake enough to warn them of consequences but still sufficiently asleep to keep them trapped in the vice. They are, in fact, complicit with the spirit keeping them hostage; they don't want to leave prison—they don't want freedom, although many would claim they do.

- *Repentance is agreeing swiftly and humbly with the Accuser.*

This practice is a protocol with many people who advocate taking a case to the Courts of Heaven. When, during that process, the Accuser of the Brethren and enemy of our souls makes a charge, we should agree swiftly and humbly with that indictment. This, for many people currently, is what *repentance* means.

Now this misunderstanding, in my view, comes from a combination of factors. It comes from a conflation of *repentance* with *confession* and then, once they are mixed together, not so much a perversion of *repentance* but of *confession*.

To *confess* simply means to *agree*. That is why we can have a 'confession of faith' and also 'confession of sin'. The first means to *agree* that, for example, *'Jesus Christ is Lord of all'* and the second means to *agree*, for example, that I sinned when I told my new neighbour a lie about the fence line.

Repentance is different. Genuine repentance actually involves restitution, if possible, but we try to wriggle out of that by invoking the mantra, 'That's Law, not grace,' when we actually should be intent on image-bearing God through simple justice. Restitution is stratospherically beyond us because it's an intense struggle just to turn back to God.

If you are using the Courts of Heaven because you can get from the Divine Judge what you cannot get from your Heavenly Father, you need to seriously examine your motivation and relationship. If you hear an accusation from the enemy and, instead of agreeing with it swiftly and humbly, are unwilling to present it immediately to the Holy Spirit, our advocate, to ask His advice on the matter, then again you need to seriously examine your motivation and relationship.

At no time in the history of the church have believers ever before confessed to the devil. Because that's what *agreeing* with his accusations actually means. And that agreement is not repentance. If we think we've repented because we've agreed with the satan, we are greatly deceived. He is the Father of lies and therefore to agree with anything He says without seeking the counsel of our Advocate is beyond unwise. It is complicity.

I've had this argument with people who actually teach others about how to approach the Courts of Heaven. I have been astonished by their adamant resistance to inquiring of the Holy Spirit or of Jesus, our other Advocate, before agreeing 'swiftly and humbly' with the accusation. They won't even try seeking counsel from either of our Paracletes, in case it upsets the protocol. I sense a fear of violating legal technicality, not a reliance on grace, in that refusal.

This is not to say there is not a place for the Courts of Heaven but with the caveat that it's wise to have actually received God's permission to go there.

I can tell my Heavenly Daddy that I'm sorry without going to court to do it. I can tell Him I've sinned and I want to get back into right relationship with Him without making a federal case out of it. I can petition Him without the Whole Big Judgment Scene happening. I can sit down with Him and go through, in excruciating detail, the choices I made that led to such painful consequences. I prefer to be closeted away with Him when I do this, not make a courtroom drama out of it.

It is never acceptable to allow the satan to call the shots or give his twisted indictments priority over the words of Jesus or the Holy Spirit. That is to give the enemy more right to speak over my life than my Friend.

- *Repentance is a 'change of mind', not a 'change of behaviour'.*

The Greek word, 'metanoia', *repent*, means *to change one's mind*. But to suggest, as some scholars now do, that this is separate from *a change of behaviour* is a classic example of Greek thinking in opposition to a Hebrew mindset.

Oh, alright, that's actually giving it too much credence, too much legitimacy. It's really just another pathetic excuse for wallowing in behaviour that God has told us to have nothing to do with. As if God's love means that He's perfectly willing to tolerate actions like abuse. No, God's love means that He's perfectly willing to give us everything we need to *stop* tolerating, enabling or enacting abuse. He's given us tools of grace so we can love Him in return with all of our heart, mind, soul and strength. He's done so at the Cross but, unless we are willing to apply the gift of the atonement, then we haven't accepted His grace at all. The atonement, the *at-one-ment*, doesn't allow us to separate ourselves from God or to separate mind from behaviour. *At-one* means *oneness, unity, communion*.

Just as James had to remind his readers that faith cannot be divided from works, so a change of mind cannot be detached from a change of behaviour. It's not that we are justified by works, but that works demonstrate the reality of our faith. So too a change of behaviour demonstrates the reality of our 'metanoia', *change of mind*.

> *Someone will say, 'You have faith and I have deeds.' Show me your faith without deeds, and I will show you my faith by my deeds. You believe that God is one. Good for you! Even the demons believe that—and shudder.*
>
> James 2:18-19 BSB

Just as saving belief in God is far more than mere assent to His existence or that He is one, so repentance is more than a change of mind. It has to flow out into action, or else it is meaningless. If the actions of a person who has changed their mind are no different than the actions of a person who has not changed their mind, then repentance is an illusion.

- ✖ *Repentance is a misunderstanding of authority; it's better to 'decree and declare'.*

Belial has his hoofprints all over this one. It involves another inversion of meaning, this time around 'authority'.

A woman had outmanoeuvred her brothers and sisters for a larger share of the family inheritance, and had then managed to inveigle several significant clients away from her business partners before launching out on her own. In time, the sowing-and-reaping principle caught up with her and, whenever she was about to close a deal, she'd be blindsided by a rival from another company. She was on the verge of bankruptcy when she sought help. She couldn't understand why so many misfortunes had occurred. In her view, God's favour had rested upon her previously regarding the setting up of her business as well as in the matter of the family inheritance.

When she was advised she was reaping what she'd sown and that it would only get worse if she didn't repent of her manipulative behaviour, she took offence. She further decided that she'd show the world. She would take up her authority in Christ and deal with the problem properly. And so she decreed and declared publicly that her business would prosper and that all of the negative words spoken against it, and her, would fall to the ground, null and void.

Her business still exists, but only just.

To 'decree and declare' in order to evade any unpleasant consequences for sin that God has spelled out in His Word is far more than a misuse of authority. It's an attempt at magic. When we use the creative, activating power God put into words to try to negate and overrule His Word, we are simply dabbling in magic.

When Jesus gave us authority, He didn't mean that we can make up our own rules.

> *I have given you authority to trample on snakes and scorpions and to overcome all the power of the enemy; nothing will harm you.*
>
> Luke 10:19 NIV

Authority is the delegated power to uphold the law according to the will of the lawmakers; it is not the power to do as we feel is right. When we exercise authority by upholding God's law and will, He backs us fully. Anything else is a misuse of the authority invested in us.

> ✓ *So what is repentance really?*
> *How is it accomplished?*

Repentance really is as simple as a change of mind that results in turning back to God. It's easy to say but not easy to achieve. We quickly find that we might be willing to repent, we might sincerely want to change our minds and turn back to God, we might even determinedly set our will to enact a full-180 about-turn, but all our best efforts come to nothing. Sin has so tight a hold on us that repentance is not just difficult, it's impossible.

Biblical repentance has overtones of burning the 'house' of your past life to ashes behind you so you can't come back to it. We have to ask the Holy Spirit with His tongues of flame to set fire to all that's gone before.

This drastic change is beyond our power. Only with the saving help of the Blood of Jesus can we accomplish it. He is our mediator, our intercessor, our conciliator, our facilitator. The Holy Spirit stirs us up to hate the sin in ourselves and Jesus gives us the means to remove it. Our part is simply to be willing enough to speak words of repentance and call on the Lord to activate what we've said. If we're genuine in our desire, He will respond. We might fail, we might waver, we might keep turning away and turning back, but He will give us the power to not give up.

Eventually repentance will become a lifestyle. But one day, as I've testified in *Hidden in the Cleft*, repentance loses its power. And on that day—on the day God says to us that repentance has become more of a formula than a relationship—He begins to expose the parts of our heart where we've adamantly and repeatedly refused Him access.

It's all too easy to adopt an attitude towards repentance that dishonours this gift of His grace. As we've just seen, some people are of the view that we cheapen grace by repenting. However, others think exactly the opposite: that we cheapen grace by not repenting.

Some people think we can make good health manifest by changing our minds and no longer thinking the toxic thoughts of the past. But putting our old behaviour behind our backs and just 'moving on' or 'building a bridge and getting over it' is not the same as turning our backs and going to God. We haven't turned away from sin in disgust, we've just let it slide into the rearview mirror.

One day, God quietly said to me, 'You need to repent of taking long baths.'

This was so out of the blue and unexpected, I responded with a baffled 'Huh? I haven't taken a bath for over twenty years.'

He repeated: 'You need to repent of taking long baths.'

'Lord,' I said. 'Would You mind explaining? I don't want to start getting super-religious or hyper-scrupulous. Why would I need to repent of having long baths?'

And He got me to understand that it was an old false refuge that still existed. The idols in it—since idols take up residence in all false refuges—hadn't vacated the premises just because I hadn't used it in decades. He made the further point that the enemy of my soul was scouring my life, looking for ways to assert legal rights and make accusations against me.

It learned from that conversation with the Lord that repentance is not simply stopping any specific behaviour, it's speaking words of turning and asking Jesus to empower them. It doesn't matter how long it's been since the last time I sought that particular false refuge. So 'moving on' or 'getting over' means nothing in the spiritual world unless it's accompanied by genuine repentance.

That that can only come through grace.

But, like the misunderstandings around repentance, there's confusion too around grace. It's all too easy to get the idea that, because we're saved by grace through faith, then the law no longer applies. We think the law has been superseded. Yet Jesus said:

> *Do not think that I have come to abolish the Law or the Prophets; I have not come to abolish them but to fulfill them.*
>
> Matthew 5:17 NIV

So, to see what He meant by this, let's make some comparisons between what Moses revealed and what Jesus said.

> Moses: don't kill.
>> Jesus: don't get angry; that's murder in the heart.
>
> Moses: don't commit adultery.
>> Jesus: don't even lust.
>
> Moses: don't steal.
>> Jesus: give to those who ask.
>
> Moses: love your neighbour.
>> Jesus: love your enemies.
>
> Moses: don't break your oaths.
>> Jesus: don't make vows; just keep your word and let your yes be *yes* and your no be *no*.

You know what? The Law of Moses is much easier than the commands of Jesus. And the Law of Moses isn't superseded in the sense that it is no longer relevant, it is superseded in the sense that Jesus raised the bar higher. He raised it to Himalayan heights and then, because He knew we couldn't even reach the lower bar set by Moses, He empowered us to keep the Law through His grace.

He did not come to sidestep the Law so that repentance is a once-for-all event that does us for a lifetime. The sacrifice of Jesus on the Cross is that once-for-all event—and our repentance, our turning back to Him and away from sin, when empowered by His grace, enables us to mature towards that Everest height of righteousness that Jesus set as His standard for the Law.

We have to keep recognising that without the empowerment of Jesus, nothing we do will be effective. He wants us to join with Him, because that's how our relationship grows, but we're not doing any of the heavy lifting when it comes to giving up our sinful habits.

Still, we deep down believe we need to *'do'* something to make a difference, especially when it's an intractable sin. Our natural human inclination to want to help Jesus out when we've prayed and prayed and prayed and nothing's changed. We wonder what else we can we 'do'? Confess? Repent? Forgive? Renounce? Trade? Go to the courts?

The truth is that we are so inventive in finding ways to enhance the atonement. Repentance and forgiveness only 'work' because God tells them to. They operate by His grace, not because we've made a choice of will. God requires them as tokens of loyalty towards Him but, in truth, they don't add a single thing to the all-sufficiency of the sacrifice of Jesus. They are more about marks of love than anything else—about telling God that, yes, broken as I am, I am committed to the relationship. And that, in my heart of hearts, I cannot believe in the atonement without wanting to *'do'* something to help Jesus solve my present crisis. Because I'd like to trust Him, but I can't.

The only fallback position in this case is, I believe, encapsulated in the words of the father who had taken his son to the shrine of the goat-god Pan: 'Lord, I believe—help my unbelief.'

To go back to the beginning. To start over.

Repentance offers us a wondrous taste of what it meant for the Jordan to roll back to Adam and for God, in essence, to say to His people, 'This is a new chance. Go into the land, and be the stewards and keepers of your inheritance in the way I intended for Adam and Eve to be My guardians and caretakers in the Garden.'

Sometimes we think that repentance is a punishment—and, if we get in first, God will be less severe with us. That's not true repentance, it's not a desire for a restored relationship, rather it's low self-esteem. It's not only dishonour of self, it's a belief in our own worthlessness. Instead of understanding that God sees us to be of such worth Jesus died to cancel the punishment for our sins, we still feel a need to punish ourselves. This is complicity with both Leviathan *and* Belial.[27]

Sometimes, on the other hand, we think that repenting is a way of appeasing God. We believe He is angry with us and, by repenting, we can get Him to turn aside from His wrath. Now, if you knew Old Norse, you'd know what a nice pun that last statement was. In the north of Scotland is

Cape Wrath, named by the Vikings as a directional marker. It means Cape *Turn-around*. Our language still preserves that tiny, tiny bit of understanding that repentance and wrath are both ways of saying *turn for home.*

When the Israelites crossed the Jordan as the waters rolled back to Adam, they weren't about to enter a primal, pristine garden. There were now thorns and thistles to contend with. And some of those thorns and thistles were cities devoted to godlings who demanded human sacrifice, particularly the offering of firstborn sons. The defilement on the land in some places was so great that Yahweh called for its total 'devotion'—that is, complete destruction of both city and people and a perpetual ban on ever rebuilding in that location. God particularly specified that this decree applied wherever the people had worshipped Belial.

> *If you hear it said about one of the towns the Lord your God is giving you to live in that troublemakers* [sons of Belial] *have arisen among you and have led the people of their town astray, saying, 'Let us go and worship other gods' (gods you have not known), then you must inquire, probe and investigate it thoroughly. And if it is true and it has been proved that this detestable thing has been done among you, you must certainly put to the sword all who live in that town. You must destroy it completely, both its people and its livestock. You are to gather all the plunder of the town into the middle of the public square and completely burn the town and all its plunder*

as a whole burnt offering to the Lord your God. That town is to remain a ruin forever, never to be rebuilt, and none of the condemned things are to be found in your hands. Then the Lord will turn from His fierce anger, will show you mercy, and will have compassion on you. He will increase your numbers, as He promised on oath to your ancestors—because you obey the Lord your God by keeping all His commands that I am giving you today and doing what is right in His eyes.

Deuteronomy 13:12–18 NIV

Yahweh had made it clear, back in Abraham's day, He would never ask for human sacrifice. So, following a godling who demanded such tribute meant the inexorable law of sowing-and-reaping would inevitably bring terrible retribution down not only on yourself but on your family too. Across three or four generations that could amount to hundreds, perhaps thousands, of people. So God's decree to destroy everything might seem immeasurably harsh, but it actually minimised the reaping by a timely intervention.

The reaping for Abraham's abuse was four hundred years of slavery for his descendants. What would the reaping be for child sacrifice? Too terrible to imagine.

Here we see why Jericho was razed to the ground and a total prohibition placed on taking any item from it. The defilement was so great it would bring temptation upon the Israelites to appease the fallen angels—the principalities, the powers, the world-rulers—with human sacrifice. Whatever the 'genius loci', *the spirit of the place,* was, it would await its opportunity, centuries down the line, to re-establish worship in blood for itself.

But, for us, the Blood of Jesus is enough for all time to overcome such dark powers.

Prayer

Abba, Father, thank You for Your gifts of repentance and forgiveness. Thank You for the blessing of Your power behind our words so that all we have to do is be willing enough to speak and be humble enough to ask You to give the words life. Teach me and remind me that repentance and forgiveness are not possible in my strength but only through Your activation of them. Allow me to sense the rejoicing of heaven over a single sinner who repents—me! Allow that downpour of joy to lift my burden of shame.

Lord, where I need to bring more than repentance but restitution, empower me to do so. Let me encounter Jesus, like Zacchaeus, so that I can be an agent of healing and peace-bringing to my entire community through justice and restoration. Remind me and remind me and remind me, Lord, that restitution is not a negation of the law but a fulfillment of it. Remind me and remind me and remind me of Your golden rule: *do unto others as you would have them do unto you.* Treat other people with goodness, kindness and faithfulness. How I can expect to reap 'chesed' if I am not willing to sow it?

Lord, above all at this moment, I ask You to prepare my heart so You can annul my complicity with the spirit of abuse, of time and of armies. Show me my false refuges, the ones hidden even from myself where I have enthroned Kronos or Belial in a small, quiet shrine behind a secret door. Reveal to me the vows I've made, the lies I've believed, the faith in the Passover of Time I didn't know I was holding to, the alliances I'm unaware of. Break down the vows and the lies, Lord, as I specifically renounce them. Cut down my faith in Your enemies and sever my alliances with them and the generational treaties of my family. Plant in me true faith in You and strengthen that faith as it grows. Help me go on well, Lord. Help me finish well.

Father, in asking for Your help to overcome Kronos, there is a continual temptation to fulfil my own personal needs, rather than ask for my community or nation. Let me be sensitive to Your appointed time for any reset and let it be according to Your will for the Body of Christ.

Lord, I have been irresponsible concerning the time given to me—help me to flow in Your Spirit through work and rest in their appropriate seasons.

> In the name of Jesus as the mighty redeemer of time and the Lord of Angel Armies. Amen.

4

The Ancient of Days

O worship the King all-glorious above,
O gratefully sing His power and His love:
our shield and defender, the Ancient of Days,
pavilioned in splendour and girded with praise.

O measureless Might, unchangeable Love,
whom angels delight to worship above!
Your ransomed creation, with glory ablaze,
in true adoration shall sing to Your praise!

Robert Grant

Why a *ram*?

Doesn't it strike you as a bit odd that, as Abraham was about to sacrifice Isaac, he saw a ram in the thicket and not a lamb? In a sort of way, it fits that it's a ram, but at the same time, a huge question mark hangs over it. If

God can perfectly arrange foreshadowings of Jesus—as He did so often elsewhere—it seems strange that here, of all places, the alignment is less than impeccable.

So is the ram pointing to something else?

Now the word translated *ram* is 'ayil', and it has a multitude of other meanings. Besides *ram*, it can be *oak, post, pillar, lintel, stag, chief* or *mighty man*, depending on the context. Basically, the thought behind it is the *strong leader*. One of the names for God, 'El', is said have the sense *almighty* and to be a contraction of 'ayil'.

Obviously, since the 'ayil' spotted by Abraham has horns, that narrows the possibilities. It comes down to *stag* or *ram*. Most people would be tempted to discount stag, but I don't necessarily think so. It would be an even earlier hint than occurs at the end of the Song of Songs about the resurrection:

> *Make haste, my beloved, and be like a gazelle or a young stag on the mountains of spices.*
>
> Song of Solomon 8:14 ESV

This is a prophecy of the 'mountain of spices' created by Nicodemus and the faithful women disciples for the marriage of the Lamb, His resurrection from the dead and His triumph over the gatekeeper of the underworld, the stag-entity Resheph—mentioned by name in that last chapter of the Song of Songs.

Tempting as I find *stag* to be, I'm nevertheless going to choose the traditional translation and go for *ram*. My reason for doing so is because I suspect that, along with all the other things hidden in this scene, ultimately it's about names. Most threshold tests are.

Names are vehicles for both identity and destiny. They carry our calling and vocation. Not in a fatalistic way, not in any sense that we are pre-destined to achieve the purpose for which God created us, but to the end that if we choose to follow God's summons, we will walk in the works He has always ordained for us.

One of the reasons God institutes a name covenant[28]—offering us either a new name or a new meaning for our old one—when He's beckoning us towards our destiny is in order to bypass the claim the satan has put in for the name we've grown up with and the destiny that goes with it. God quickly follows up with a threshold covenant because we desperately need Him as our covenant defender so that the satan does not snatch our new calling from us.

You may remember that, besides *laughter*, Isaac also has several other resonances.[29] These include *lintel, cloud, thin covering, third heaven, glory*. It's easy to overlook *lintel* in that line-up; it's more than overshadowed by *third heaven* and *glory*. Importantly, one of the meanings of 'ayil' is *lintel*. Regardless of whether the 'ayil' is a *ram* or a *stag*, it qualifies as a substitute for a *lintel*. So, when Abraham saw the 'ayil', he immediately recognised its substitutionary nature for someone named Isaac.

But does the ram tell us more? I'm inclined to think so.

The deity associated with the ram was Baal Hammon, who was worshipped by the Phoenicians. The name 'Phoenicia' is, in fact, simply a classical Greek term for the port cities of the Canaanites. Baal Hammon was often pictured with curling ram's horns and his name means *lord of the brazier* or *lord of the incense altar*[30] or *lord of a multitude*.[31] His heyday was in Carthage in North Africa during the fifth century BC, after that colony broke away from the Phoenician mother-city of Tyre.

Baal Hammon was more commonly known as Melqart, *king of the city*,[32] and was known to the Israelites as Moloch, to the Greeks as Kronos or Cronus, and to the Romans as Saturn. Despite the popularity of Baal Hammon peaking in the fifth century BC, I think we can safely push the date for his worship back at least another thousand years closer to the time of Abraham. In the distribution of land inheritance for the tribe of Asher, their territory included a border village in the vicinity of Tyre called Hammon.[33] This has been identified as Umm el Awamid, just south of Tyre, where two Phoenician inscriptions mentioning the worship of Baal Hammon have been found.

The possibility that Hammon means *multitude* gives a direct link to Abraham's name, traditionally meaning *father of a multitude*.[34] Abram doesn't contain the element 'ham', *multitude*, but Abra*ham* does. What we seem to be looking at here is a counter-claim to Yahweh's covenant with Abraham—a counter-claim by Hammon-Moloch-Kronos-Saturn-Belial, each and all of whom demanded child sacrifice. The legal right to pursue this test would have come through Abraham's continued alliance with the spirit of abuse—whichever one of the faces of Hammon, Moloch, Kronos, Saturn, Belial or any other godling that it was.[35]

This suggests Mount Moriah was a site associated with a Canaanite godling, not with Yahweh. In later times, it became the site of the threshing floor that David bought from Araunah, who was probably king of the Jebusites. But perhaps it was *always* a threshing floor, even in Abraham's time. Threshing floors, after all, were often surrounded by man-made thickets to stop large animals like goats, sheep, oxen and deer foraging on the heaps of grain temporarily stored there. A ram wouldn't normally get caught in a thicket unless it was trying to get through some undergrowth to some food.[36] Wheat or barley would be an especially luscious and tempting target.

More importantly, however, is the significance of threshing floors. Amongst other things, they were seen as portals between heaven and earth. For the Amorites in the time of Abraham and later also in David's time for their descendants, the Jebusites, a threshing floor was the ideal place to conduct pagan rites of divination and necromancy.

The fact that David secured it as the future site for the Temple doesn't automatically wipe away its historical association with abuse or with the rituals that had taken place there. In fact, though it's dangerous to read backwards in Scripture and to invest the past with an understanding taken from a different age, there is nonetheless no question that particular locations can become defiled and that patterns are repeated across time.

So consider: David acquired the threshing floor that was once Mount Moriah from Araunah. He did so after seeing an angel of destruction, halted at that very spot before the gates of Jerusalem, with a plague-sword held aloft in his hand. The angel was stationary because God had commanded:

> *'Enough! Stay your hand!'*
>
> 2 Samuel 24:16 ISV

Can you hear the distant echo of the past in these words? Abraham was at this very same site, holding a knife aloft and about to offer Isaac, when the Angel of Yahweh told him in very similar terms to stop.

> *'Do not stretch out your hand.'*
>
> Genesis 22:12 NASB

The destroying angel who stopped on the threshold of Jerusalem had brought plague on the land as a direct consequence of David's sin in ordering a census of the fighting men. David had had a long time—nine months and twenty days—to repent of his failure to trust God and call the census off, but by the time his conscience awoke, it was too late. He'd been warned, right at the beginning, by no less than his army commander Joab—hardly the most spiritually sensitive of men—that this headcount was unwise in the extreme. Now if Joab could pick it, anyone could. David had been tested and found wanting.

And although Abraham was tested and not found wanting, there are sufficient parallels in their stories to strongly reinforce the possibility that Abraham's test at Moriah is also connected with enduring sin. With, as I've said, complicity with the spirit of abuse.

Who was David then complicit with? My guess would be the spirit of armies. And those entities—the spirit of armies and the spirit of abuse—are one and the same. It's no surprise then that when abuse occurred in David's family, he behaved exactly like Abraham did when confronted with Sarah's mistreatment of Hagar: nothing.

David's daughter Tamar was raped by her brother Amnon and, when David heard about it, he ignored it. He pretended nothing had happened. He failed to call Amnon to account for the sexual molestation of his sister and he failed to send for Tamar to comfort her and show her acceptance and reassurance. He abandoned his daughter, offering her neither justice nor mercy. She was a tragic figure, unable to marry, mired in grief.

The defilement on the landscape, the contamination by the spirit of abuse, started in the time of Abraham and continued, in my view, century after century after century. It persisted down to the time of David and went on beyond that era, right down to the time of Hezekiah. That corruption and lack of cleansing is, I believe, exactly what Isaiah is implying is the issue when He speaks of God laying a Cornerstone in Zion. Why would God need to place one there when there already was one? The only reason would have to be that there was something wrong. That Jerusalem actually needed a new Cornerstone, precious and pure.

And, when God arranged for that to happen, there would be—of course—a reset of time.

The Cornerstone is critical to the reset. It appears in each story of Time turning back, sometimes at the rollback, sometimes just a few days beforehand. Now it's not always obvious that a cornerstone is present. It's one of those things that didn't need to be mentioned for an ancient reader to know it was there.

Before the Sea was pushed back, there was the first Passover. And that Passover automatically involved a cornerstone: that's because the people were told to paint the lintels and doorposts with blood. As it dripped down, the blood would pool in the shallow basin carved into the cornerstone on the threshold. Anyone 'passing over' the blood on the cornerstone came into covenant relationship with the householder; a covenant that naturally included an agreement of mutual defence. The blood around the doorway at the original Passover was the sign of an invitation to God to 'pass over' the cornerstone, to stay for the prepared feast of lamb and bitter herbs, and also to defend the family in the home where He'd joined in the supper.

The second element that is critical to a reset is the Cloud. We see the protective cloud pillar appearing between the Egyptian armies and the Israelites as they travelled towards the Sea.

These same two elements, the Cornerstone and the Cloud, appear in the story of Joshua asking God to pause Time during the battle with the five armies. The cornerstone is found at the Ascent of Beth Horon—the pathway between the two parts of the first city built by a Hebrew in the Promised Land. The Cloud covering has to be there because of the hailstorm or meteorite shower.

Once again, as I've suggested, the same elements appear after Isaiah prophesies that the Assyrian threat will come to nothing because of the new cornerstone laid in Zion and the covering Cloud that obliterates the invading army.

And they are present at the crucifixion, when a very mysterious timewarp occurs. Jesus Himself is of course the Chief Cornerstone and it is the Passover, the anniversary of the original divine covenant, when God 'passed over' the cornerstones of the Hebrew houses in Egypt. Darkness was the covering over the land at the time of the crucifixion. Luke describes it as an *eclipse*—though, technically, that is impossible. If he used *eclipse* in its scientific sense, the positions of the moon and the sun cannot be explained. For a solar eclipse, the only possible way one can occur during the day, is for the moon to be between the earth and the sun. And, at

Passover, it's always on the far side of the earth—in the worst possible position. Besides, a solar eclipse only lasts a few minutes, not three hours, not from 'the sixth to the ninth hour'.[37]

Luke might have been using the word *eclipse* in a more literary sense, since he does this elsewhere.[38] In that case, it means *to leave off, to stop* or *to cease*. This is very similar to Joshua's command for the sun to stop—and so perhaps Luke used it in order to evoke that ancient miracle of the stopping of Time.

Here, not far from the Temple constructed on Araunah's threshing floor that had previously been Mount Moriah, Jesus died and was buried. Prior to His death, He'd been through a series of illegal trials, He had been abused and mocked by Roman soldiers, He'd been subjected to torture, He was ridiculed by onlookers and was surrounded by tormentors.

In one of those perverted switches that Belial specialises in, the crowds had shouted for the release of the murderer and rebel Barabbas while baying for the death of the innocent Son of Man, Jesus. Spiritually He was hemmed in on every side by 'bulls of Bashan'.

All the faces of the spirit of abuse were there. The spirit of armies was in attendance. The spirit of time, the elder-god who wants to eat the future, was there trying to consume the greatest destiny of all: that of the Saviour of all mankind.

But God was preparing the greatest reset of all: the resurrection. It was set to take place at a specially appointed time: the Feast of Firstfruits.

> *He will speak out against the Most High and oppress the saints of the Most High, intending to change the appointed times and laws; and the saints will be given into his hand for a time, and times, and half a time.*
>
> Daniel 7:25 BSB

In Daniel's vision of the court of the Ancient of Days, he sees a terrifying spectacle of God's people being oppressed by a *'beast that crushed and devoured its victims and trampled underfoot whatever was left'*[39] and that defeated the saints of God *'until the Ancient of Days came and pronounced judgment in favour of the holy people of the Most High, and the time came when they possessed the kingdom.'*[40]

The 'Ancient of Days', the 'Ancient One', is a title for God as the Sovereign King from everlasting. Although the description of the Ancient of Days is all-glorious light—dazzling white clothes and hair as white as wool—the image that sticks in the minds of many people is of a greybeard Judge who punishes us for every infringement of the Law. In fact, the Ancient of Days is a Judge who protects people from abuse by limiting the power of the oppressor.

Counterfeiting the Ancient of Days is the Greek titan Kronos or the Roman scythe-wielder Saturn, called the 'old god' or 'elder god', and who also has an association with days. Saturday was named for Saturn. Originally Chronos, the Greek time-lord, was not the same as Kronos but they were conflated quite early, so I don't intend to differentiate between them.

Kronos, in Greek mythology, was the son of Uranus, *heaven* or *sky*, whom he deposed by castrating him. Or, as has been poetically put, he cut heaven. Perhaps it's an attempt to pervert covenant, since it seems so like, and yet so different from, the covenant sign of circumcision. Kronos was a titan, a giant. On being warned by his father that he would reap what he'd sown—well, not in those exact words of course but that's what Uranus meant—Kronos feared he'd be overthrown by one of his children. So, as soon as they were born, he swallowed them whole. Eventually Zeus was born and hidden away before Kronos could dispose of him and, when he grew up, tricked Kronos into regurgitating his brothers and sisters. Zeus then embarked on a long, bitter war against Kronos and the titans that finally eventuated in their defeat. They were then incarcerated in Tartarus, the netherhell.

This is where, according to Peter, the fallen Watchers are confined.

> *God didn't spare the angels who sinned but threw them down into Tartarus and delivered them to be kept in chains of darkness until judgment.*
>
> 2 Peter 2:4 HCSB

We tend to think of the titans and their successors, the godlings and goddesses of Olympus, as the stuff of myth, legend and folklore. But the early church did not think this way. Nor did Jesus. He was in constant conflict with a realm of supernatural entities who claimed dominion over the world.

Derek Gilbert points out: 'The preachers, teachers, and theologians of the early Christian church were nearly unanimous in the belief that the gods of the Greeks and Romans were not imaginary, as most of us modern Christians assume. They, like the Jewish scholars a few hundred years earlier, understood that the Olympians, Titans, Gigantes, heroes, and *daimones* of the pagans were supernatural beings called "angels," "Watchers," "sons of God," "Nephilim," "Rephaim," and "demons."'[41]

In fact, the earliest description of Kronos doesn't describe him as a giant. He doesn't even have flesh or a physical body. He was 'envisaged as an incorporeal god, serpentine in form, with three heads—that of a man, a bull, and a lion.'[42] 'Serpentine' suggests a *seraph*, since that word for a six-winged throne guardian actually means *fiery snake*. But the description of the three heads is so very reminiscent of one of the cherubim as Ezekiel initially[43] portrays them:

> *The form of each of their faces was that of a man, and each of the four had the face of a lion on the right, the face of an ox on the left, and the face of an eagle.*
>
> Ezekiel 1:10 HCSB

These are *faces;* while the account of Kronos specifies *heads*. In other words, some being with faces like one of the cherubim but with multiple heads like Leviathan. And Leviathan too has influence when it comes to a 'day'.

When Job was wishing he'd never been born, he spoke of the *day* of his birth:

> *May those curse it who curse the day, those who are ready to arouse Leviathan.*
>
> Job 3:8 NKJV

It doesn't matter how many times I read that verse from Job, I still think *no*. I have trouble coping with the idea, even though I've now encountered too many people who've had the day of their birth cursed and whose life stories show they have been marked for backlash from Leviathan from that point on. But something in me still wants to resist the possibility it is so simple to rouse Leviathan and target the innocent. Yes, I struggle—but I don't disbelieve.

Many people, however, discount any thought that Leviathan can inflict a lifetime of retaliation on a believer because of the protection of the Blood of Jesus. The reality is that the Blood of Jesus empowers us to achieve those impossible things—repentance and forgiveness—but it does not allow us to continue in complicity without consequence. And it's all too easy to be complicit with dishonour when it's all we've ever known.

> *There, the ships pass through; Leviathan, which You created, frolics in it.*
>
> Psalm 104:26 ISV

Leviathan was created to laugh and play in the deep, to display joy and usher us into God's presence with courtesy and honour. Its natural element is 'yam', *the sea*. As we've seen, there's a curious connection between yam, *sea*, and yom, *day*.

Perhaps when we curse a day, we also curse the sea—and Leviathan, feeling the defiling effects and sensing the pushback against the frolicking joy it is responsible for maintaining, reacts with a stinging lash. I'm just guessing at a mechanism. Maybe it's a lot simpler. Maybe it's just that if we dishonour a 'day', ultimately we are dishonouring God, the creator of the Day. And if someone dishonours a day in our name and we, through relentless mind control over us, come into agreement with that, then Leviathan has the right to payback. We're triply in trouble: we've dishonoured a Day, we've dishonoured its Creator and we've agreed with the dishonour meted out to us.

What is the answer to this threefold cord of dishonour? God's grace, of course! That wonderful gift of grace called *repentance*, along with that other marvellous sign of divine favour, *forgiveness*, are given to us to set things right. Forgiveness and repentance, when empowered and activated by the Blood and the Cross of Jesus, bring us back into relationship with God and others.

It doesn't matter who or what we dishonour. We cannot dishonour anything or anyone—not even something as 'abstract' as a DAY. There is nothing in God's creation—including its fallen aspects and beings—that we are allowed to revile, curse or abuse. Believers who engage in spiritual warfare are apt to forget—or ignore, because of a mistaken belief that their authority supersedes the Word of God—what both Jude and Peter said about abusing and reviling fallen angels:

> *These people have visions which make them... despise God's authority and insult the glorious beings above. Not even the chief angel Michael did this. In his quarrel with the Devil, when they argued about who would have the body of Moses, Michael did not dare condemn the Devil with insulting words, but said, 'The Lord rebuke you!'*
>
> Jude 1:8–9 GNT

Rebuke: the sense of the word in Greek is to *pay back honour for honour*. Presumably that also implies *dishonour for dishonour,* as well. I totally see why this is such a safe prayer to address to the Father. The only spiritual legal right a fallen power can claim over us from this petition is to boomerang the rebuke: *to return honour for honour, dishonour for dishonour*. And if we haven't dishonoured anyone, or have repented of dishonour, then only honour can be paid to us. What threshold guardian is going to exercise the right to ask God for His favour to dwell ever more richly on us?

'The Lord rebuke you!' is a declaration that de-claws the enemy. But many people find it difficult to surrender the authority they believe they possess into the Lord's hands. 'I rebuke you!' is the compromise some believers reach, still clinging to that idea of authority as delegated power to enforce their own will, rather than delegated power to uphold the will and Word of God.

'Time is an illusion,' said Albert Einstein. Certainly the theory of relativity makes time curiously flexible—to the point that it disappears entirely for any object able to travel at the speed of light. What that means is that, we can look at a star—say, Alpha Centauri, the closest neighbour to the solar system at about 41,200,000,000,000 kilometres[44]—and realise the light took about four years and four months to reach us. However, from the point of view of the light itself, *no time whatsoever* would have elapsed. It doesn't matter how far distant a star is, or for how many ages the light has been journeying towards us from our perspective, from the point of view of the light itself, *no time whatsoever* elapses.

On the one hand, time flows by at a 'normal' rate for us while the photons of light interact with eternity. We can change the 'normal' rate by increasing our speed but we don't currently have any practical way of doing that in order to make any appreciable difference in practice.

Until recently—before we began to measure time using atomic clocks—we used mechanically-geared timepieces for all everyday purposes. These were divided into twelve hours of sixty minutes, with the minutes subdivided into sixty seconds. The definition for a second was defined in these terms: there were 31556925.9747 seconds in the tropical year 1900. Not especially practical for common, daily use. Even less practical is the present definition: the duration of the second is 9192631770 vibrations of the unperturbed ground-state hyperfine transition frequency of the caesium-133 atom.

So let's go back to the sixty seconds in a minute and sixty minutes in an hour. Those sixties might seem strange but they are very ancient in origin. They come from the days of the Babylonian magi, where they were tied in with angular measurement. The mathematics of the magi was based around the number 6, as well as 60 and 360. We still retain the Babylonian system of angles with 360° in a circle, along with one degree subdivided into sixty minutes and each minute in turn made up of sixty seconds.

For the magi, both time and angles were interconnected through their common dimensions: sixty minutes, each of sixty seconds. It's likely this originated in astronomical observations. More than one ancient calendar system has 360 days annually, so the possibility that this was actually once the length of a year cannot be discounted. Since, after all, Joshua's command to the sun and the moon to stand still is effectively an order to stop the earth's rotation or else tilt its axis—and I have to wonder what physical means was used to accomplish that: a large comet in close proximity, thus explaining the meteorite bombardment?—it's natural there should be a flow-on effect to the length of a year.

The 'prophetic year'—the length of a year as used in prophetic pronouncements—was in line with this older calendar of 360 days. And there were, of course, other calendars. The lunar calendar annually runs to 354 days and only lines up with the solar calendar every 19 years.

In the various different testaments about Enoch where astronomy and calendric measurement are featured, the most common theme is the count of the year as 364 days, one day short of an ordinary solar year, perhaps because it's an exact multiple of 7. Enoch, of course, is associated with both angels and Watchers. The English word *watcher* is itself a time-associated word. A *watch* for the wrist was developed so that those 'on watch', particularly in the military, could accurately mark the time period assigned to them for observation. There's that very faint aroma of warfare attached to it, reminding us that the spirit of time is also a spirit of armies and a spirit of abuse.

In most of the world today, we use the Gregorian calendar—named for Pope Gregory XIII who, in October 1582, instituted a reform of the Julian calendar which had been used since the first century BC when it was introduced by Julius Caesar. Utterly appropriate endeavour for someone who'd adopted the name Gregory because it means *the watcher*. Nevertheless the Julian calendar is still currently used in some places: the Berbers use it, so do some Christian churches in Ethiopia and Syria, and most notably, it's used by Eastern Orthodox churches of Jerusalem, Serbia, Montenegro, Poland, North Macedonia, Georgia, Ukraine and, of course, Russia—where Christians famously celebrate the Feast of the Nativity, 'Christmas', on 7 January.

Most curiously, the Julian calendar is used for dating in astronomy.

Now this may seem like an odd question, but here goes: which calendar operates in the spiritual world? I wouldn't even think to ask this question except that many years ago, when I was first beginning to realise the ancient biblical notion that names encoded destiny was actually true, I noticed something extremely peculiar during my research. Sometimes I'd have to explore the ramifications of a saint's name (who would have imagined, for example, that a name like Christopher would be a sanitisation of a legend about the Norse godling, Thor?) and I began to realise that many people encountered their most serious obstacles in life either on their 'name day' or else ten or eleven days later.

A 'name day' used to be much more important in certain European communities than a birthday. It still is, in some places. Some people may never have celebrated their actual birthday, only their 'name day'—the feast day of the saint after whom they were named.

What I quickly realised was that if people experienced trouble *on* their 'name day', the issue they were dealing with was 'recent'—that is, if it had any generational component, it went back only a century or so. If there was an 11-day phase delay, the issue went back before 1582. And if it was a 10-day discrepancy, the matter dated to between 1582, when the Julian calendar was adopted across most of Europe, and 1752, the year when Britain adopted it.

You may ask: what's this problem with 'name days'? It's simple. The satan has claimed all names. He was cast out of heaven for trading in names[45] and with their associated identities, destinies and callings. If a name is attached to a day, he's claimed the day as well. Of course he has. God's sovereignty over each day is under constant challenge on multiple fronts.

That is why we are asked by the Lord to steward each day as part of our inheritance and to look to Jesus as the Redeemer of our wasted time.

I, the Lord, tell you that these prophets have never attended a meeting of My council in heaven or heard Me speak.

Jeremiah 23:18 CEV

To be a true prophet means that we must have stood in the Divine Council and heard God's decrees. Jeremiah delivered the Lord's denunciation of false prophets by revealing that they'd never attended a Council meeting. To enter the courts where God presides, the spirit of a prophet visits the realms of eternity. Visions in that space have a sense of immediacy that are not congruent with time back in our mundane world. I'm sure Isaiah had no idea many of his prophecies would not be fulfilled for hundreds of years; in fact, we're still waiting on some.

Of course there are some prophecies that do come to pass immediately: the shadow on the stairs of Ahaz. Or at a precisely designated time: Jeremiah's prophecy that the exile in Babylon would end after seventy years, a prophecy that Daniel felt needed fasting and prayer to see its fulfillment.

And then, of course, there's Micaiah's prophecy that Ahab would die at Ramoth Gilead. Because of all the aspects of threshold covenant in the story, it's worth quoting that particular Scriptural passage in detail:

> *Jehoshaphat king of Judah went down to visit the king of Israel, who said to his servants, 'Do you not know that Ramoth-gilead is ours, but we have failed to take it from the hand of the king of Aram?'*
>
> *So he asked Jehoshaphat, 'Will you go with me to fight against Ramoth-gilead?'*

Jehoshaphat answered the king of Israel, 'I am like you, my people are your people, and my horses are your horses.' But Jehoshaphat also said to the king of Israel, 'Please inquire first for the word of the Lord [Yahweh].'

So the king of Israel assembled the prophets, about four hundred men, and asked them, 'Should I go to war against Ramoth-gilead, or should I refrain?'

'Go up,' they replied, 'and the Lord [Adonai] *will deliver it into the hand of the king.'*

But Jehoshaphat asked, "Is there not still a prophet of the Lord [Yahweh] *here of whom we can inquire?"*

The king of Israel answered, 'There is still one man who can ask the Lord [Yahweh], *but I hate him because he never prophesies anything good for me, but only bad. He is Micaiah son of Imlah.'*

'The king should not say that!' Jehoshaphat replied.

So the king of Israel called one of his officials and said, 'Bring Micaiah son of Imlah at once.'

Dressed in royal attire, the king of Israel and Jehoshaphat king of Judah were sitting on their thrones at the threshing floor by the entrance of the gate of Samaria, with all the prophets prophesying before them. Now Zedekiah... had made for himself iron horns and declared, 'This is what the Lord

[Yahweh] *says: "With these you shall gore the Arameans until they are finished off."'*

And all the prophets were prophesying the same, saying, 'Go up to Ramoth-gilead and prosper, for the Lord [Yahweh] *will deliver it into the hand of the king.'*

Then the messenger who had gone to call Micaiah instructed him, 'Behold now, with one accord the words of the prophets are favourable to the king. So please let your words be like theirs, and speak favourably.'

But Micaiah said, 'As surely as the Lord [Yahweh] *lives, I will speak whatever the Lord* [Yahweh] *tells me.'*

When Micaiah arrived, the king asked him, 'Micaiah, should we go to war against Ramoth-gilead, or should we refrain?'

'Go up and triumph,' Micaiah replied, 'for the Lord [Yahweh] *will give it into the hand of the king.'*

But the king said to him, 'How many times must I make you swear not to tell me anything but the truth in the name of the Lord [Yahweh]*?'*

So Micaiah declared: 'I saw all Israel scattered on the hills like sheep without a shepherd. And the Lord [Yahweh] *said, "These people have no master; let each one return home in peace."'*

Then the king of Israel said to Jehoshaphat, 'Did I not tell you that he never prophesies good for me, but only bad?'

Micaiah continued, 'Therefore hear the word of the Lord [Yahweh]*: I saw the Lord* [Yahweh] *sitting on His throne, and all the host of heaven standing by Him on His right and on His left. And the Lord* [Yahweh] *said, "Who will entice Ahab to march up and fall at Ramoth-gilead?"*

And one suggested this, and another that. Then a spirit came forward, stood before the Lord [Yahweh]*, and said, "I will entice him."*

"By what means?" asked the Lord [Yahweh]*.*

And he replied, "I will go out and be a lying spirit in the mouths of all his prophets."

"You will surely entice him and prevail," said the Lord [Yahweh]*. "Go and do it."*

So you see, the Lord [Yahweh] *has put a lying spirit in the mouths of all these prophets of yours, and the Lord* [Yahweh] *has pronounced disaster against you.'*

Then Zedekiah... went up, struck Micaiah in the face, and demanded, 'Which way did the Spirit of the Lord [Yahweh] *go when He departed from me to speak with you?'*

Micaiah replied, 'You will soon see, on that day when you go and hide in an inner room.'

And the king of Israel declared, 'Take Micaiah and ... put this man in prison and feed him only bread and water until I return safely.'

But Micaiah replied, 'If you ever return safely, the Lord [Yahweh] has not spoken through me.' Then he added, 'Take heed, all you people!'

So the king of Israel and Jehoshaphat king of Judah went up to Ramoth-gilead. And the king of Israel said to Jehoshaphat, 'I will disguise myself and go into battle, but you wear your royal robes.' So the king of Israel disguised himself and went into battle...

A certain man drew his bow without taking special aim, and he struck the king of Israel between the joints of his armour. So the king said to his charioteer, 'Turn around and take me out of the battle, for I am badly wounded!'

The battle raged throughout that day, and the king was propped up in his chariot... and that evening he died. As the sun was setting, the cry rang out in the army: 'Every man to his own city, and every man to his own land!'

So the king died and was brought to Samaria, where they buried him. And the chariot was washed at the pool of Samaria... and the dogs licked up Ahab's blood, according to the word that the Lord [Yahweh] had spoken.

1 Kings 22:2–38 BSB

The king of Judah had gone on a state visit to the kingdom of Israel. He'd accepted the hospitality of King Ahab, meaning that he'd undertaken a threshold covenant. We can be sure of this because of what happens next. Ahab suggests that they go to war together against Aram. This put Jehoshaphat in a bind.

Threshold covenant entails an obligation to mutual defence and, in fact, very few statements ever express the oneness of this commitment as well as Jehoshaphat's words: *'I am like you, my people are your people, and my horses are your horses.'* However in an attempt to wriggle out of this particular trap, he requested: *'Please inquire first for the word of Yahweh.'*

Ahab sent for his four hundred prophets. Now, those four hundred prophets simply should *not* have been there. They are obviously replacements for the four hundred prophets of Baal killed by Elijah at Mount Carmel.

Before we go on, it's long past time for a reminder.

No one is good, except God alone.

No one. Not even Elijah.

It's incredibly difficult for many people, regardless of whether they are Christian or Jewish, to read the narrative about Elijah with objective eyes. So many believers idolise him that they don't notice how blatantly he defied God. Had Elijah done as God instructed him—anoint Jehu and Hazael as kings—then Ahab would have been deposed years previously. The incident at Naboth's

Vineyard *would* never have occurred and *should* never have occurred. The 'sons of Belial', the worshippers of the spirit of abuse who accused Naboth of blasphemy and had him stoned to death, would not have been hired by Jezebel—because Jezebel would have been long gone.

We discover Elijah's negligence when Jehu is driving like a maniac into Samaria just after he's finally been anointed by a member of the company of the prophets who had been sent by Elisha. Jehu reminds his chariot driver, Bidkar, that they'd been riding behind Ahab when they'd heard the prophecy that Ahab would pay for the blood of Naboth and his sons on the very plot of ground Jezebel had conspired to acquire. But that prophecy was given by Elijah! This means that, even after the tragedy of Naboth's Vineyard and even after he had actually met up with Jehu, Elijah still didn't take the opportunity to obey the Lord.

Ahab's rule extended far beyond the time the Lord had allotted for it. Two of Ahab's sons in succession assumed the throne of Israel when it should have gone to Jehu. Elijah's disobedience cost lives. He knew the will of God and ignored it.

But Elijah, despite his repeated claim that he was the only prophet left, was far from alone. There were several unnamed prophets who confronted Ahab after the Mount Carmel incident and there was, by Ahab's own testimony, a prophet who never had anything positive to say. That suggests Micaiah and Ahab had had more than one face-to-face confrontation in the past.

However, before Micaiah was called, Ahab got his four hundred tame prophets to make their predictions. They are all in agreement: 'adonai', *the lord*, will cause Ahab to triumph.

Jehoshaphat was obviously alert enough to the ambiguity in the word 'adonai'. It's one of those titles that could be used deceptively. So he wriggled a bit harder to try to get out of the trap he was in and specifically asked for a prophet of Yahweh.

The two kings moved to the threshing floor near the city gate while waiting for Micaiah, son of Imlah, to arrive. There are two threshold symbols here: the city gate and the threshing floor which, as a place for divination to contact the Baals, was considered a portal between heaven and earth. Zedekiah, one of the false prophets, had figured out what Jehoshaphat needed to hear. So, putting on a pair of iron horns, he spoke in the name of Yahweh. The other prophets joined in the chorus, also making declarations in the name of Yahweh.

Now these were prophets of Baal. They didn't have the slightest authority to speak in Yahweh's name. They were lying. The spirit of Jezebel, the spirit of tearing-truth-apart, the spirit of forgetting, the spirit of Ziz—whatever name you like to call the lying spirit by—was deliberately invited down from the Council of Heaven to that threshing floor.

Micaiah arrived, prophesied victory, and Ahab immediately pulled him up. It was the first positive thing

Micaiah had ever said about him so he was instantly suspicious. He'd seen through the lie, straight away. Now there's much more here than the ability to spot a falsehood. Ahab had been set a test and he passed it. He could detect a lie from Micaiah, so it follows he could have detected a lie from Zedekiah. Especially since it was the same lie. So if he didn't confront the prophets of Baal on their false predictions, he was complicit with their lies and with the spirit behind them.

Micaiah then went on to explain the truth. He related a vision of the Divine Council that featured Yahweh commissioning a lying spirit to speak through the mouths of the four hundred prophets. It's a strange scene because lies and truth are so finely juxtaposed in it. God had permitted a lying spirit to go to earth and lure Ahab to his death. But He'd also allowed Micaiah to reveal the truth.

It wasn't as if Ahab was without knowledge of the agenda of the lying spirit. Nor was he ignorant of God's will. Nor was it as if he couldn't repent—he'd done so previously because of Elijah's dire prophecy and the Lord had spared him at that time. So he knew what the choices were. It also wasn't as if the prophets of Baal were puppets in the hands of the lying spirit—they invited its presence by speaking in a name they had no right to invoke.

Thresholds are about choices. The tests that we face on the thresholds of life, particularly as we approach the doorway into our calling, are determined by a group of fallen heavenly powers who want us to fail. Sometimes we may pass so effortlessly we aren't even aware we've been tested. Yet sometimes the test may be so grim and stressful, we are in agony even contemplating it. The difference—as a general rule—comes down to our level of complicity with the spiritual examiner. When all's said and done, that spirit is simply testing our loyalty to the One we profess to serve.

Prayer

Abba Father, Lord and Holy One of heaven, I'm sorry.

I see in the lives of David, Abraham and Elijah that complicity starts with doing nothing. It begins with realising others are being abused and with choosing to step back, deciding to not intervene, resolving to stay right out of the situation. But, actually, that's not staying out at all. It's siding, by default, with the abuser and perpetrating an alliance with the spirit of abuse, Belial. The longer I do nothing, the more time I choose to be a silent observer of another's torment, the deeper my cooperation with Kronos becomes.

I'm sorry for doing nothing. Forgive me.

I see too that, as time progresses and my complicity with Kronos grows, my trust of You, Father, dwindles. Instead of operating in faith, I protect myself with small deceptions. And instead of repenting when I see the serious consequences of those lies and half-lies, deliberate ambiguities and concealments of critical information, I repeat the deceptions. I double-down in rationalising my behaviour. My heart grows harder, especially when my deception has brought me great reward.

Then, when I am tested, I have nothing to fall back on but myself. I don't have You because I've chosen not to trust You. The enemy tests me and betrays me at one and the same time. And I sabotage myself.

In desperation I reach out for You, even while I'm still holding hands with the spirit of abuse. Kronos retains his hold on me because I'm so afraid to let go and risk the fall into Your arms. I'm not sure You'll catch me. So I'm stuck with and in Time because I am so uneasy about unconditional surrender to You. I want to choose to walk in the eternal NOW of Your presence but the implementation of that choice is beyond my capability. Help my unbelief.

Lord, there are times when I'm tempted to agree with my boss and my superiors, and to speak outside of my authority just like the false prophets did. Just as they knew what Ahab expected of them to keep their positions, I've known just what has been expected of me. Lord, I repent of the times that fear kept me from speaking truth in Your name, when it caused me to speak deception in Your name, when it prompted me to keep silence. I repent of the times I dishonoured Your name. I ask Jesus to empower my words of repentance and grant me the courage to be like Micaiah and stand against the crowd.

Lord, strengthen me to keep covenant with You and no other.

> In Jesus' faithful name. Amen.

5

Fruit that Lasts

THE FRUIT OF THE SPIRIT SEEMS an unlikely flashpoint for a war. Quite possibly you haven't noticed the conflict. The war is so covert that even those who know it is raging don't often recognise how significant Fruit is to the struggle.

I was at a conference dinner one year not long ago when the conversation at the table I'd joined turned diabolical. Some attendees, all representing a single religious group, began to express their loathing of another denomination. The hatred was open, overt and palpable. Strangely, they damned the denomination as a whole, rather than individuals.

The following year, at the next conference dinner, I made sure to steer myself to the far side of the room away from that particular clutch of specialists. I joined another table. But, to my shock, I found myself living through almost a word-for-word rerun of the previous year. The new group I'd joined were repeating exactly the same things I'd heard before, with the same vehement hatred.

I was stunned. Because here were two sets of people, from entirely different—in fact, diametrically opposed—ends of the denominational spectrum who had, as far as I could see, only one thing in common: they both detested a third denomination with an intense passion.

And those reviling insults were returned with a vengeance. I'd already heard sufficient sermons in that third denomination slamming the first religious group to know that.

As I came away from the second conference, pondering the strangeness of the conversations I'd overheard two years running, I heard a whisper from the Holy Spirit regarding the first two denominations, 'There is one other thing they have in common. They both emphasise the Fruit of the Spirit above all else.'

And I instantly realised what the contrast was. The emphasis of the third denomination is so heavily on the Gifts of the Spirit that the Fruit may as well not exist. There was, it seemed, no middle ground. This is a deep tragedy on so many levels, because both Fruit and Gifts are required in order to be able to follow Jesus and complete the work the Father has prepared for us to do. The Gifts are needed to be able to pursue our calling, but the Fruit is needed to be able to access our calling in the first place.

The Fruit is not simply a set of fine virtues or essential character-builders, comprising even more than the 'badge' by which true believers in Christ may be identified, as the Lord Himself pointed out:

> *'By their fruit you will recognise them. Not everyone who says to Me, "Lord, Lord," will enter the kingdom of heaven, but only the one who does the will of My Father who is in heaven.'*
>
> Matthew 7:20–21 NIV

The Fruit is, in addition, as I've testified in each book in this particular series, *weaponry*. Each one of them is expressly designed as an *armament* to assist us in overcoming a particular threshold spirit. Specific Fruit elements are not interchangeable as far as targeting one of the threshold guardians is concerned. You need to deploy the right Fruit, and that depends both on the circumstances and the identity of your attacker.

To mobilise against the spirit of Python, love is effective. We should target Ziz, the spirit of forgetting, with joy. It's best to overcome Leviathan and Resheph with peace, *shalom*. And to master Azazel, the spirit of rejection, as the Lord tells us to do—not cast it out, but *master* it—we need self-control, better translated as *spirit-empowerment*.

The three-in-one Fruit required to stand against both Belial and Kronos are goodness, kindness and faithfulness. Three-in-one because, behind these three English virtues, is one Hebrew concept, 'chesed'. It's so difficult to translate that Myles Coverdale resorted to inventing a new term, *lovingkindness*. But Coverdale's word is now seen as so old-fashioned that modern translators have turned to renderings like love, unfailing love, steadfast love, loving devotion, mercy, faithful love, gracious love, loyal love, favour or kindness. None of them are really adequate.

Chad Bird says: 'What is chesed? That beautifully untranslatable word for the covenantal, faithful, ferocious love of God, the kind of love that chases after us in Psalm 23 like the Hound of Heaven... the "chasidim" are the people of "chesed". The "chasidim" are those marked, set apart, and named by the love of God.'

When 'chesed' is used of God, that's a wonderful description. But when 'chesed' is used of the Fruit of the Spirit maturing in us, what does it look like? It's tempting to choose another inadequate description, *integrity*, though really it's an aspect of 'shalom'. Yet there's a certain sense in which integrity is a vital aspect of any confrontation with Belial and Kronos.

When Joshua was fighting against the five armies on the Ascent of Beth Horon, as well as against Belial and Kronos, he was armoured in integrity. He could have ignored the call for help from the Gibeonites and justified his lack of response as payback for their deception. But he didn't. He went all-out to keep covenant, even marching through the night to their aid.

Loren Sandford points out that, without the character of Christ, without the Fruit of the Spirit, we will become abusers.[46] So God calls us to integrity, to defend the defenceless, not to defend the indefensible.

He calls us to faithfulness. The only way we can demonstrate that particular Fruit is through constant fidelity *over time*. Faithfulness comes about through endurance. Through choosing God *time after time* during the highs and lows, ups and downs, mountains and valleys, bright sunlight and deep darkness. It keeps on keeping on, whatever the circumstances. Of course, we fall, we stumble, we wander in circles, we make mistakes and some of them are deliberate—but, so long as we repent and turn back to God, heaven rejoices. Faithfulness is not about perfection; it's about allegiance. It's about covenant loyalty. It's about repeatedly choosing to go back to God, failure after failure, *time and time again.*

Faithfulness, ultimately, is a gift of grace. I'm sure it would be absolutely inconceivable to Paul, writing in the first century that, two millennia on, faith without faithfulness would be a commonplace concept.

Nearly a century ago, Dietrich Bonhoeffer alerted us to 'cheap grace'—'the preaching of forgiveness without requiring repentance, baptism without church discipline, Communion without confession, absolution without personal confession. Cheap grace is grace without discipleship, grace without the cross, grace without Jesus Christ, living and incarnate.'

So too, within the formula of cheap grace, we've come to expect faith without faithfulness.

How can we realistically expect God to honour such a bizarre belief? Faith without faithfulness is a relationship without commitment. Faith without faithfulness revolves, in part, around the assumption that God shouldn't care if we're spiritually promiscuous or if we're having an affair with His enemies. The rationalisation goes that He's too loving to do anything other than shower us with intimate blessings, regardless!

Just this week I heard a new justification for lying—at least it was new to me. It goes like this: the greatest commandments in the Law are to love God and love your neighbour. So it follows that truth is insignificant compared to love, and therefore as long as we keep on loving, it doesn't matter how many lies we tell. That's a serious mangling of Jesus' directives in the cause of avoiding repentance. We're afraid of repentance because, to choose it, means that we'd have to face the real giant we don't want to acknowledge: shame.

John Bradshaw says shame lies at the root of all addictions. And behind shame is hidden pride.

Repentance is a renewal of faithfulness. It means returning to the heart of God. But it also means that there are no detours into the enemy's camp along the way.

Faithfulness is not only a Fruit of the Spirit, it is inherent to God's nature. He matures it in us, precisely in order that we may safely pass over the perilous threshold into our calling. But we have a part to play too. We have to be willing to be committed solely to Him. We have to choose to back our faith with faithfulness. We have to set our faces and decide on the long obedience in the same direction.

Grace is a gift to help us be faithful. It would have been absolutely unimaginable to the apostle Paul that his emphasis on the grace of the gospel would be, in this present age, sometimes be interpreted as God's blindness to sin. There are two ways 'grace' is used as a term in Paul's writings: one, as the unmerited favour of God and, two, as the empowerment of the blood of Jesus to overcome sin. Grace is God's offer: 'I will give you absolutely everything you need to overcome this sin. Everything—in case that isn't clear, beloved, I mean: all, without counting the cost, without measure and with no time limit.'

Can you see Belial's hand at work when 'grace' means we can go on sinning with impunity? What Belial is saying is that you can be friends with God while partying with His enemies and supporting their agenda of destruction and harm. After all:

> *where sin abounded, grace abounded much more.*
>
> Romans 5:20 NKJV

Apparently this is not a new tactic. Belial has trotted it out before and it must have been working quite well in first century Rome for Paul to address the issue so comprehensively.

What shall we say then? Shall we continue in sin that grace may abound? Certainly not! How shall we who died to sin live any longer in it?

Romans 6:1–2 NKJV

Sometimes we repent, or forgive, because we think we have to 'appease' God, to buy Him off with good behaviour and prompt obedience. We're not relying on His grace if this is our attitude. Instead we're trying a sacrifice of sorts to placate Him, or to impress Him with our willingness to obey. And of course God wants us to forgive and repent. But not in our pitiful, fleshly mechanisms that eventually frustrate us with their futility.

God wants us to forgive and repent through the power of the atonement of Jesus. He wants the at-one-ment of covenant to be the source of our authority, not the concessions of contract. When we fail to repent, God sometimes doesn't answer prayer because, in reality, we're asking Him to make us comfortable in our sin, rather than help us out of it. That's why, when decreeing and declaring have become a way of avoiding repentance, God will put a 'hold' on the timing for fulfilment.

I was once asked to co-lead a team by a very experienced mission director. Puzzled, I asked him why he wanted to parachute me in to fill the vacancy, rather than raise up one of the existing members of the team. It was because I was 'completely reliable', he said. And he went on to ask me about the people I might bring on to the team with me: were they 'reliable', 'mostly reliable' or 'unreliable'?

I was so taken aback I asked him for his definition of these categories. It turned out that 'reliable' meant someone who either did the task or, if circumstances prevented them from completing it, they would give at least a week's notice of their inability. On the other hand, 'mostly reliable' was someone who started the task the night before it was due and got most of it done on time. Anyone else was 'unreliable'. He then went through a list of over seventy names, slotting the people concerned into those categories. Six of them were 'reliable' or 'mostly reliable'.

Since that illuminating discussion, many years ago now, I've discovered that leader was basically right to suggest that about ninety percent of people fall into the 'unreliable' category.

Even me.

For some people I have a reputation of being utterly reliable, but for a long time, it was completely the opposite with many other people. It took a while to discern the difference and much, much longer to discover the spiritual roots behind the problem. If I said 'yes' and did the job, then people saw me as completely reliable. If I said 'no' and didn't do it, then I would find that I was considered unreliable. More than once, I was placed on an event roster, even after I had specifically stated I could not attend because of a prior commitment.

I realised I had a deep problem when I spoke to one leader after a weekend event. I'd asked her why she had thought I would be able to complete several tasks not assigned to me. Six weeks before the event, I had informed her that it would not be possible for me to complete the list of jobs required and, if she couldn't take on two or three of them herself, she needed to find someone else to do them.

Why, I asked afterwards, hadn't she told me she hadn't found anyone until three days beforehand? I could have found a willing helper myself if I'd known in better time. Her reply stunned me. 'I didn't want anyone else to do those jobs and I knew you didn't mean it,' she said. 'I knew you meant *yes*. I knew you'd do them. And you did.'

She was right. I actually had done them. When I discovered these advertised programme items hadn't been prepared, I dropped everything else I was organising and got them ready. As a consequence, they were done badly. So were the nearly-finished tasks I'd dropped at the last minute as well. It looked like I was the one to blame for letting hundreds of people down.

My reputation for unreliability notched up another level but, fortunately, this leader had spelled out for me what I'd only vaguely suspected in other areas of my life. My 'no' did not mean *no* as far as other people were concerned. It meant *not now*. That's how others took it.

Eventually, I was receiving prayer ministry when one of the intercessors pointed out that, during my childhood, an attempt had been made to hand on an unholy legacy to me. 'Have you forgiven the person for attempting to pass a spiritual mantle to you?' the intercessor asked.

'I didn't realise there was that aspect to it until this moment,' I said.

'Are you willing to forgive and repent of your involvement with this?'

'Repent? But I didn't accept the spiritual mantle. I said *no*.'

'*No* is not enough. You have to renounce it.'

As soon as the intercessor said, '*No* is not enough,' I knew he was right. That was my life story: *no was never enough*.

'You need to renounce the mantle,' the intercessor said. 'Renouncing is stating *forever no*.'

Ever since that day, I've been slightly into overkill when it comes to renunciation. Because after that day, *no* has indeed been enough.

The threshold guardians of the spirit world are legalists in the most excruciatingly fine technical sense. That's why I so often say to my two Paracletes, Jesus and the Holy Spirit, 'I don't know the word here to cover every aspect of this. Jesus, when You present this prayer to the Father, please rectify any inadequacies and fill in omissions and delete anything less than honouring.'

You see, there's a whole chasm of difference between giving something up and repenting of it. We can decide to control our violent rages but never repent of them. In fact, I know people who did just that. Anger was a useful tool for getting their own way—this had been the old-school managerial style of their parents and they'd taken it on, lock, stock and barrel, for more than employees. For family and friends as well. But anger tended to quickly wither those relationships. So they made a conscious effort of will to stop the outbursts of fury. And succeeded.

Yet this is not repentance. And the family knew it. It's a pragmatic, practical solution designed to contain the natural consequences of sin. It's not sorrow for harm; it's not grief over the wounds inflicted; it's not sadness over the ongoing pain.

Just stopping a behaviour is not always the same as turning your back on it, repenting of it, and facing the Cross in the hope of complete renewal and restoration. Because just as you decided to stop, so you might decide to start again. If you deem it useful to do so. It's not exactly a formula for trust.

But repentance sings a different tune. It's an aria of faithfulness to God, not a whistle of faith in ourselves.

Reliability is not a Fruit of the Spirit, but it is a facet of faithfulness. It's also a facet of integrity, 'shalom'. In addition, it's a facet of truth, 'alétheia', the art of *not forgetting*. It's also a facet of self-control, *Spirit-empowerment*. And, too, it's a part of love and honour.

An acquaintance was crazywild in love with a man who was never on time. He was always late—and not just very late but excessively late. He found it difficult to hold a job for any length of time, he rarely kept appointments—unless the person he was meeting was also running late, he held people up constantly as they waited for him to arrive. The acquaintance stuck with this guy for years, through thick and thin, defending him through the constant barrage of criticism, loving him with unparalleled devotion, sure that he just needed encouragement to change. Finally, she realised he never would and, in tears, broke off their engagement. The crunch-point came when her fiancé was asked to be the best man at a wedding. He was, unwisely, given the rings. And he arrived four hours late at the ceremony, laughing and unapologetic.

Reliability in matters of time is about the honour and respect we accord to other people. If we don't want to reap what we sow in terms of wasting the time of others, we need to honour them. To thereby show love.

Reliability is therefore a key component of love, truth, peace 'shalom', faithfulness 'chesed', self-control. And once we recognise truth, *not forgetting,* as built up by thanksgiving which in turn builds up joy, we realise reliability is one of the fertilisers that makes so many of the Fruit of the Spirit grow.

However when we are complicit with Kronos, reliability can be obsessional or alternatively erratic. It's no good being reliable if it counts more to us than relationship—

that's obsession. Nor is it any good being erratic—because who can count on us to keep our word? Can God rely on us to pursue His calling for us?

When we haven't approached Jesus to help us master our unreliability or even our obsessional reliability, we will be tempted to abuse and misuse Him as Lord of Time. We are not to call on Him to show Himself strong as Lord of Time just because we didn't start an important project until the night before it was due.

The stories of Joshua calling on God to stay the sun and moon, and of Isaiah asking the shadow to turn back, of the Jordan heaping up at the town of Adam, and of the Sea rolling back, are all stories that are national in scope.

We are meant to ask God for help against Kronos on behalf of the nations, not for our own personal convenience. That's why we are called to stand in His heavenly council: not for ourselves but for the world.

Faithfulness, goodness and kindness are all wrapped up together in a three-in-one spiritual Fruit. One of the finest tricks in the arsenal of the spirit of abuse—as well as the other threshold spirits—is to get us to believe that we should never judge others. This is another one of those mind traps and thought reversals designed to confine believers who want to stand against abuse. If we fall for it, we give abusers ever greater room to perpetrate harm.

Controllers always remind us that the people of God who are His carriers and distributors of goodness and kindness should always bear in mind the words of Jesus:

> *'Do not judge, or you too will be judged.'*
>
> Matthew 7:1 NIV

Now, the way this verse is often interpreted—that we should never question anyone's motives or have doubts about their behaviour or truthfulness—would mean that Jesus contradicts Himself in His very next sentence.

> *'For in the same way you judge others, you will be judged, and with the measure you use, it will be measured to you.'*
>
> Matthew 7:2 NIV

It's actually about reaping as we have sown. The measure we use will be measured back to us. In the context of the previous chapter and the three verses following, it becomes clear that Jesus is teaching about different aspects of hypocrisy.

> *Why do you look at the speck of sawdust in your brother's eye and pay no attention to the plank in your own eye? How can you say to your brother, 'Let me take the speck out of your eye,' when all the time there is a plank in your own eye? You hypocrite, first take the plank out of your own eye, and then you will see clearly to remove the speck from your brother's eye.*
>
> Matthew 7:3–5 NIV

In the previous chapter we had:

- 🕀 don't give to charity, like the hypocrites do (Matthew 6:2)
- 🕀 don't pray, like the hypocrites do (Matthew 6:5)
- 🕀 don't fast, like the hypocrites do (Matthew 6:16)

These commands explicitly mention hypocrisy,[47] though the previous chapter is full of implicit teaching on it too. Jesus says not to swear an oath, but to let our *yes* be *yes* and our *no* be *no*. This was because the lawyers at the time had become adept at creating technical loopholes so that the rich could evade repaying debts or honouring their vows. Their dodgy practices included such evasions as 'the oath is not binding because it was only *by the altar*, not *by the gift* on the altar' and other similar stratagems. No wonder Jesus said to simply keep our word.

The discussion on adultery and divorce is amplified by a later question of the Pharisees:

> *'Is it lawful for a man to divorce his wife for any reason?'*
>
> Matthew 19:3 NIV

Back in the time of Jesus 'for any reason' or 'for any cause' had the sense: because he feels like it. It's not asking if there are specific reasons when divorce is allowable; it's asking if any specious reason will do. Is it permissible for a man, bored with a woman, to cast her out and find a newer model? Again, it's all about hypocrisy.

This is how we are to judge. We are not to condemn others in a hypocritical way. We must do it with integrity. We must apply the same standards to ourselves that we apply to others. That's what Jesus is saying.

Because of course we are to 'judge'. Have we forgotten already that no one is good except God alone? Every day we have to make critical decisions, involving judgments between right and wrong. That's the essence of choice and freewill. Jesus Himself told the crowd to 'judge' correctly, not by appearances (John 7:24), and Paul asked the Corinthians to 'judge' for themselves (1 Corinthians 11:13).

I repeat: of course we are to 'judge'. Do you think God wants us to put our children in harm's way by ignoring all our instincts and allowing them to be alone with people we sense are dangerous and abusive?

If we can't judge, then how are we to forgive? Because forgiveness presupposes that a judgment has been made. That judgment essentially is: 'You have chosen to do the wrong thing and have caused me harm.' But I now choose to forgive you.

If we can't judge, then how are we to repent? Because repentance presupposes we have made a judgment on ourselves. We agree with God that we've done wrong and we choose to change.

Prayer is asking God for a judgment in our favour. The Hebrew language actually recognises this: 'palal', *pray, entreat* or *ask*, is also a word for *shaking* and for *judgment*.

Goodness, kindness and faithfulness cannot be separated from judgment. They can be separated from condemnation, however.

Why is Belial so intent on convincing us that we ought never judge another? Why do the other threshold guardians back him so relentlessly on this? The answer is simple. So we don't judge them.

As we approach the threshold into our calling, we need to discern whether the sentinels waiting there are hostile or protective. This is part of what it means to judge angels. (1 Corinthians 6:3) Another part of that calling is to uphold the sentence God has already pronounced over them. We are not authorised to pass sentence on them, nor are we authorised to dishonour them in any way. For fallen angels, our task is very simple because they must reap what they've sown. There is no hypocrisy about judgment in the Kingdom of Heaven. It's the same rule for them as for us.

Yet, there is no redemption for the angels. In the previous book in this series, I looked at the most likely reasons why. These reasons are precisely the same as the ones that resulted in such fatal consequences for the Israelites who turned against God after celebrating the first Passover—that threshold or cornerstone covenant that altered their relationship with Him, moving it beyond family to include friendship. But that new bond, as we noted, also opened up a new possibility: in families, you disobey; in friendships, you betray.

Sedition takes relationship-shattering to an entirely different level. The throne guardians who rebelled against God and tried both to corrupt and to pre-empt His plans for the redemption of humanity committed high treason against Him, precisely because they were so close to Him and were aware of His intentions. The principalities who followed in their footsteps after they were given governance of seventy nations following the scattering from Babel likewise betrayed their high calling.

And when we have accepted threshold covenant and then gone on to betray our high calling, we cannot expect an indulgent smile and a token chastisement. We are talking deliberately and callously turning away from our own exemplary record of faithfulness, goodness and kindness in order to become like the abusers we've opposed in the past. Now by 'exemplary' I don't mean 'perfect'—what I mean is that if we've made a mistake, we've admitted it and repented of it.

The reason why the fallen angels put so much effort into stopping us crossing over the threshold is that, if we can move freely around in that space, we can actually sit at the gates. And that is exactly what a judge did in ancient times. In fact, 'gates' and 'judges' became synonymous. We displace the unholy angels at the gates and become judges ourselves. It's not as if we have to stretch ourselves to judge those angels: there is only one ruling we can speak out and it is already decreed for us in Psalm 82. These angels have caused death and corruption of nature. Therefore their own nature will be subject to decay and they will die.

It's important for us to learn how to judge righteously. Not in condemnation but in goodness, mercy and truth. We have to go to Jesus and confess, 'No one is good but God alone but I need to be good in order to combat the spirit of abuse and of time and of armies. Only if You cover me in Your goodness through the atoning power of Your Blood can I possibly be who I need to be. I ask for that covering, that Cloud of glory above and that precious Cornerstone of a sure foundation below. I wait for You, Lord.'

The stories of Belial and Kronos involve attempts to anticipate, pre-empt and obstruct the plans of God by tempting us to do things out of time and contrary to divine timing. The inscription on the cornerstone in Zion is:

Whoever believes will not be in haste.

Isaiah 28:16 ESV

As indicated in *Dealing with Belial*, the Cornerstone and the covenant associated with it are critical aspects in our protective covering against the armies of the spirit of abuse. Though *'not... haste'* on the inscription is probably the most efficient translation, it nevertheless doesn't quite convey the right impression. It implies slowness and may even give the idea of leisure. In fact, a much better image would point us to the Feast of Sukkot, the annual time of intentional tabernacling with God, a state of waiting in rest and joy, as well as watchful preparedness. Relaxed but alert.

Do not be in haste tells us to work to God's appointed time, not get ahead of Him through any sense of urgency. Kronos or Belial might well stress us into a rush so that we, like them, pre-empt the seasons of God. If that sense of urgency is so compelling you cannot shake it, then ask God to:

- ⏱ give you the empowerment to remove your false refuges
- ⏱ repent of hidden sin and unconscious complicity
- ⏱ then to set you under His Cloud with a new Cornerstone
- ⏱ give you extra time, like Joshua and Isaiah, to defeat your enemies.

And if there's not enough time to do all these preliminaries—for they are a process and they do take considerable time—then ask for His grace anyway. Commit yourself to doing the things you need to do, if God in His grace gives you the time, slightly out of its timing.

But if you make this commitment, then be sure to keep it. Let your *yes* be *yes* and your *no* be *no*. Anything else is of the evil one. Do not mock God's grace by failing to keep your word.

Getting ahead of God is one thing. Lagging behind His timing is quite another. Sometimes we fool ourselves that we're 'waiting on the Lord' when really we're just stuck. We think we're learning patience but actually we're scared to move on. We're not faithfully following His Cloud, we've plopped ourselves down on the desert sand somewhere and we're hoping He'll just teleport us into Eden. We don't want any more thresholds, or threshold guardians, or tests, or temptations. Just a table of delights in a five-star tabernacle.

The Tartars of Mongolia have a curse: 'May you live forever in one place—and work like a Russian.'

There's a sense of security in being tied to one place—but that's not God's plan for us. He wants us to grow and expand and move with Him to fresh pastures and new territories. He wants us to take back and mend the world that we've been appointed to judge. Part of the judging process is determining what needs to be fixed and petitioning God for the resources to accomplish it.

There's a surprising word in Hebrew whose root meaning is *to be permanently fixed in one place:* it's *grumble*.

When we grumble, we're not praising. When we complain, we're not giving thanks.

Remember what happened when the Israelites grumbled in the fortieth year of their desert wanderings? Their dishonour of God brought retaliation from the 'nachash'—a seraph like Leviathan. When we fail to give thanks, we soon forget the good and find we've invited a spirit like Ziz to be with us.

But when we praise God, He comes to inhabit our praises and tabernacle with us. Yes, He's Immanuel, always with us, however the paradox is that we still need to invite Him in. When we grumble, we're wanting to stay comfortably just where we are. We're resistant to following Jesus, the Redeemer of Time, to sailing away with the wind of the Spirit and to journeying forward when the Cloud moves on.

The Feast of Tabernacles is, as I have pointed out in *Dealing with Belial,* a time when Jesus was repeatedly involved with water-drawing ceremonies. During one of these He proclaimed Himself the 'Living Water' and His words express His desire for everyone who thirsts to come to Him—they further imply He is offering healing from trauma.

Trauma, like grumbling, pins us in one place: the *past.* But Jesus wants to remove the out-of-time attachment to a particular time and heal our wounds, giving us rest and joy. It is no coincidence that one of the water-drawing ceremonies associated with joy was the wedding feast at Cana. It was held during the festival of Sukkot, the Feast of Tabernacles and we should not be at all surprised to realise it's all about time.

The incident at the wedding in Cana reveals something extraordinary about God. We really should know this all along from the story of Joshua and the sun standing still, but it's easy for some of the nuances to escape us. In Joshua's story, the time is not right—there's not enough of it. In the wedding story, the time is not right—Jesus is not ready to 'go public'.

> *When the wine ran out, Jesus' mother said to Him, 'They have no more wine.'*
>
> *'Woman, why does this concern us?' Jesus replied. 'My hour has not yet come.'*
>
> John 2:3-4 BSB

And yet, Jesus goes ahead and performs a miracle anyway. Many people suggest that God never changes His mind, although Scripture is full of instances and incidents that say He did. This is just one of those occasions—and each of them have something in common. Someone, usually a prophet, went to the Lord and asked Him to change an outcome that was about to befall the nation. In this case, it's Mary, asking on behalf of a wedding party. And, as God did for the prophets, Jesus does for Mary—because, as God, relationship is more important to Him than matters of timing or authority.

People think God would never change His mind because that would indicate a loss of authority. This is thinking in human terms about power structures. However, God can never lose authority. He *is* authority.

Yet He places a priority on relationship. Cana means *reeds*. For the Hebrews, *reeds* were not only symbolic of thresholds—they mark the transition from land to water, and are a reminder of the greatest of historical thresholds, the crossing of the Sea of Reeds—they also denote brotherhood. Relationship. Family.

When Jesus responds to Mary's request, He shows Himself more concerned for people than for any aspect of 'right timing'. Yet, paradoxically, even as He ignores 'right timing', He shows Himself as Lord of Time. The miracle of water-into-wine is about timing. There's actually nothing very unusual about water changing to wine—every day, along grape vines, water and sunlight and trace minerals combine to form bunches of fruit that will eventually be picked and made into wine. God changes water into grapes for wine on a daily basis—but the normally process takes months. Jesus did it in minutes.

Jesus repeatedly said that He only did what His Father did—and, as pointed out in *Dealing with Belial*, there's a profound difference between turning water into wine and turning stones into bread. One is a miracle, the other is magic. One keeps within the boundaries of a species-kind, the other transgresses it entirely.

Belial wants us to transgress kinds, to break down the boundaries between species, to bend and break the distinctions between the different 'kinds' that God appointed in creation. Most of the threshold spirits don't want us to cross thresholds, but Belial does. Python is intent on crushing us before we can pass over, Ziz doesn't even want us to remember there is a threshold at all, Rachab wants us waste all our energy so it's impossible to make it across.

But Belial wants us to transgress thresholds—he wants us to be the cause of our own ruination. He wants us to become his image-bearer, and not God's, and he wants us to do that by doing as he did. He wants us to cross a forbidden frontier just as he did when he trespassed across the boundary God had put in place between humanity and angels. Kronos, Belial's alter-ego, is classed as one of the titans of Greek mythology. Although we usually think of 'titan' as meaning *giant* and although it was used to translate the Hebrew word *nephilim*, it actually means the *one who oversteps boundaries*.[48]

In engineering the existence of an angel-human hybrid by mating with women, Belial altered the genetic structure of our singular 'kind'. This imperilled the redemption of humanity, since God's promise of a saviour actually required 'humanity' to exist.

God isn't interested in our race or ethnicity, despite what some people may think in reading the stories of Ezra and Nehemiah. When the Jewish people returned from exile to Jerusalem, some of them married foreign wives. Ezra and Nehemiah urged the men to divorce these women and send them and their children away.

Many people, both historically and in the present day, think they did the right thing. But is this harsh choice a right one? Whatever the case for pure bloodlines, should the consequences be to make children fatherless? Should it be to abandon mothers without means of support? Isn't that abuse?

Now, despite Nehemiah's obvious sincerity, we can't class his actions as *good* just because he was a man of integrity. Within the Fruit of the Spirit, there is peace, *shalom*—integrity, and also goodness. Although they obviously should go together, we can't assume integrity equals goodness. Nor can we, as I've pointed out repeatedly, assume that God approves of an action just because it's recorded in Scripture without a negative comment. We have to look carefully sometimes to see the consequences in a later age before we can determine God's views on the matter.

Now Jesus didn't ever *say* this decree of Ezra and Nehemiah was wrong. But His actions speak louder than any lecture. He simply went to talk with a foreign wife who'd lost five husbands and chose her as His first evangelist. He spoke to her about Living Water—which heals trauma[49]—and about time:

> *'But a time is coming and has now come when the true worshippers will worship the Father in spirit and in truth, for the Father is seeking such as these to worship Him. God is Spirit, and His worshippers must worship Him in spirit and in truth.'*
>
> John 4:23-24 BSB

Perhaps when He approached this woman, Jesus remembered how many foreign women were in the bloodline of David: Tamar and Rahab, both Canaanites, and Ruth, a Moabite. In fact, David's wives were mostly foreign as were Solomon's wives. Bathsheba may have been a Hittite, like her first husband. Further along the royal line, there was Athaliah, the queen mother, who slaughtered all but one of the heirs to the kingdom of Judah and briefly took over the throne when her son was killed. Her mother was Jezebel, the wife of Ahab and the daughter of the king of Tyre—which means that the most notorious foreign queen in Israelite history features in the genealogy of Jesus.

In addition, Moses had a foreign wife, Zipporah, and a second foreign wife who was Egyptian. Samson had two foreign wives, one of whom was Delilah. Esau also had two foreign wives. Judah had a foreign wife, Shua. Joseph had a foreign wife, Asenath. Joseph's eleven brothers almost certainly had foreign wives. Elijah was sent to a foreign woman for help.

On the other hand, God at times told the Israelites to completely wipe out certain tribes and nations, women and children included. Why the apparent contradiction? What does it say? Is racial purity important or not?

One of the things that the nations destined for destruction have in common is the presence of *rephaim* or *nephilim* ancestry. Their DNA had been contaminated by the giants, the titans, the demi-gods. Consistently in Scripture, it is the *humanity* of the bloodline that is important to God, not *race* or *culture* or *ethnicity*. The wifely purity that God required for inclusion in His chosen people is actually that the woman be 100% human, not 100% Jew.

So what should Ezra and Nehemiah have done? Simple: they should have given the foreign women the choice of

Ruth and Rahab—to covenant with Yahweh and stay; or not and leave. The decision would then have been theirs.

Jesus doesn't simply meet with a Samaritan woman at a well, He enacted a covenant with her and her community. He stayed with the Samaritans for two days—indicating He had accepted their hospitality and become their covenant defender. Moreover, because the Samaritans proclaimed Him as the Messiah, the kingdom that had split in the time of David's grandson was reunited.

This is what *good* means. To heal the wounds of history.

Yes, it's true no one is good except God alone. Yet, He still calls us to that high estate. But how can we practise goodness if it's unreachable? We can do so through the grace of divine covenant and the power of the atonement. That is exactly what the covenantal oneness of atonement is for: to be in Christ and He in us. His power will be available so we can stand against the assaults of the enemy. His power will ripen all the Fruit of the Spirit to maturity within us so they are ready to be deployed against God's enemy and the enemy of our souls.

Prayer

Abba Father, You are wonderfully kind and generous. You shower us with gifts that, however we abuse or misuse them, You will never ask for them back. Have I thought of myself as better than others because of Your undeserved grace to me? I repent, Lord, of exalting myself, mistaking the honour You have granted me for a sign of worthiness in myself.

Abba Father, You are immeasurably merciful and loving. You give us the Fruit of the Spirit and wait for us to partner with You so that the Fruit can mature and grow. The Fruit needs Your light to fructify, and stern challenges for the tree to become hardy, and the wind and water of Your Holy Spirit to grow plump and flavoursome and my cooperation with Your work as the Gardener. I can hide the Fruit in darkness, I can refuse every challenge, I can erect barriers against the Spirit's wind and water. In short, I can allow the Fruit to wither rather than flourish. Help me, Lord, to choose Your character and to become agile with the Fruit as Your weaponry. Help me not to despise either the Gifts of Your Spirit or the Fruit of Your Spirit but to know the right place of each in my life.

Thank You for being the Gardener who wisely prunes me, so I don't grow lawless and wild, but so the flavours of Your grace are ever-sweetening in my life, and the fragrance of Your love flows through me to others.

Help me not to despise Your grace or to take it for granted. Never allow me to casually dismiss sin because Your grace will cover it. Your grace is so precious—Your boundless favour and Your activating power to change. When I am tempted to rationalise my behaviour instead of repent, remind me of Your call to be transformed, forgive, be reliable, discern, and judge without hypocrisy but in a righteous blend of justice and mercy.

In Jesus' name. Amen.

6

The Garden Beyond Time

WHEN MY SISTER WAS VERY YOUNG, she heard the story of the assassination of the Roman emperor Caligula. It distressed her greatly and she decided to pray for Caligula—and for his horse, of course. The fact that Caligula had been dead for nearly two millennia wasn't relevant in her view. She reasoned that God is the Lord of time and that answering such a prayer is no harder to Him than making water run uphill.

Or, I now think, causing it to roll back upstream.

When the Israelites crossed the Jordan and the river banked up back at Adam, God's invitation to reset the time back to Eden was implicit in what happened. This was not the only time God sent out an invitation of this type:

> *Fifty men from the company of the prophets went and stood at a distance, facing the place where Elijah and Elisha had stopped at the Jordan. Elijah took his cloak, rolled it up and struck the water with it. The water divided to the right and to the left, and the two of them crossed over on dry ground.*

When they had crossed, Elijah said to Elisha, 'Tell me, what can I do for you before I am taken from you?'

'Let me inherit a double portion of your spirit,' Elisha replied.

'You have asked a difficult thing,' Elijah said, 'yet if you see me when I am taken from you, it will be yours—otherwise, it will not.'

As they were walking along and talking together, suddenly a chariot of fire and horses of fire appeared and separated the two of them, and Elijah went up to heaven in a whirlwind. Elisha saw this and cried out, 'My father! My father! The chariots and horsemen of Israel!' And Elisha saw him no more. Then he took hold of his garment and tore it in two.

Elisha then picked up Elijah's cloak that had fallen from him and went back and stood on the bank of the Jordan. He took the cloak that had fallen from Elijah and struck the water with it. 'Where now is the Lord, the God of Elijah?' he asked. When he struck the water, it divided to the right and to the left, and he crossed over.

2 Kings 2:7-14 NIV

The images of threshold are many: a portal opening into heaven, a whirlwind of Cloud, a long-established Cornerstone at the Jordan crossing, and a vision of what seems, from Elisha's cry, to be angelic armies. As we've seen from the armies, the Cloud and the Cornerstone in the stories of Joshua and Hezekiah, this combination also suggests there is some component of Time involved.

So if a reset of time is going on here, what is it about? Can we find any clues in Elisha's request for a double portion of Elijah's spirit? Perhaps it's not such an outrageous request. Perhaps it's simply Elisha asking to be recognised as Elijah's 'firstborn'. A firstborn son, after all, would be entitled to a double portion of an inheritance in order to fulfil his responsibilities towards the economic security of the wider family, particularly the unmarried women and widows. But what does it mean to ask for a double portion of someone's *spirit* as an inheritance? Perhaps Elisha was asking—at least I *hope* he was asking—for permission to complete the tasks Elijah had left undone. We've already noted Elijah's negligence in regard to Jehu. But he was also negligent in regard to Hazael—the commander God had asked Elijah to anoint as king of Aram. He simply never obeyed God's direction in this regard. Given that he had the opportunity with Jehu and failed to take it up, we have to conclude this matter of Hazael was another deliberate omission on Elijah's part.

I believe that Elijah simply didn't *want* God's choices when it came to replacing the kings of Samaria and Aram. Jehu and Hazael were ruthless and violent; Ahab was urbane and civilised. Jehu was a tough soldier, manic when it came to chariot-driving. He commanded a frontier fortress, while Ahab lived in a palace tiled in pearl. Elijah had several talks with Ahab, once persuading him to repent—but it seems that, even when the opportunity presented itself, he avoiding talking to Jehu.

All this suggests it wasn't just failure on Elijah's part regarding the change of government. It was calculated defiance of God.

Never forget: *no one is good except God alone.*

But God wants us to be good, to fulfil His purposes for the world, to advance His 'chesed' in our community and in our nation and right around the globe. He's always looking for the right opportunity—the right timing—to give us another chance. So, perhaps the time reset when Elisha crossed back over the Jordan was meant to take the kingdom back to that critical moment of choice when an angel cooked breakfast for Elijah.

Elijah had just fled from Samaria. The great confrontation with the prophets of Baal and Asherah on Mount Carmel had culminated with fire coming down from heaven to consume the offering intended for Yahweh. The people had turned back to God; the false prophets had been killed; the drought had broken; rain had come to the land.

Jezebel, on hearing the fate of the prophets who ate at the king's table, swore that Elijah would end up like one of them. Actually, let's look at her exact threat:

> *May the gods* [elohim] *deal with me, be it ever so severely, if by this time tomorrow I do not make your life like that of one of them.*
>
> 1 Kings 19:2 BSB

Something in those words transformed Elijah's elation to fear, spiking him into a panic that was accompanied by a downward spiral of depression. Something in those words ultimately caused him to forsake his calling and never take it up again. After examining Jezebel's threat closely for a very long time, the only thing I can see as a source of terror is actually the word 'elohim', *gods*. In context, it's probably not any old gods, it's probably the brothers of Baal Hadad, one of the deities Elijah had just defeated. In my view, Jezebel had just called up 69 other principalities, the 'young lions' of Mount Hermon, who would have a vested interest in avenging their mother and brother—Asherah and Baal Hadad.

Now, just as we can tell what God's intention was for Ezra and Nehemiah when it came to marriage with foreigners because of the actions of Jesus, I believe we can also tell what God's intention was for Elijah after the triumph on Mount Carmel. And it wasn't to flee for 46 days, right down to Beersheba and from there to the mountain of 'ha'elohim', Horeb in the Sinai. It was to change the government.

But by the time Elijah had left Samaria and dashed headlong through the Kingdom of Judah, six days had passed. He'd dismissed his servant at Beersheba, gone into the desert and sat down under a broom tree, moaning to God that he wanted to die. After falling asleep, he woke up to find that an angel had cooked him breakfast—there was bread baking on hot coals waiting for him.

I'm going to interpret what happens next in the light of the only other occasion in Scripture when someone is running away from his calling and a breakfast of bread baking on hot coals is a significant part of the story. The runner was Peter; he'd just given up the 'fisher of men' task he'd been called to and had gone back to his former profession as a fisherman. Someone on the beach, baking bread and fish on hot coals, calls out and directs him to a catch of 153 large fish. That someone is Jesus who, with three questions, turns Peter back to His calling.

Because of this, I believe the breakfast cooked for Elijah by the angel of Yahweh was not intended to sustain him for a further forty days as he journeyed to Horeb—it was to give him the strength to go back to Samaria and change the government. Ahab's steward, Obadiah, was a faithful believer and was daily risking his life to save 100 prophets of Yahweh who were holed up in two caves where food and water was being supplied to them.

There was a spiritual power vacuum in Samaria with the prophets of Baal and Asherah gone. Had Elijah gone back and ushered those prophets of Yahweh out from the caves and into the court as advisers to the king, the entire country would have changed. Was he meant to do this? Absolutely! Again, based on what Jesus did, we can see what God intended on this earlier occasion.

God eventually told Elijah that he wasn't the only one left, despite his repeated assertion this was the case. God revealed there were 7000 people who had not bowed to Baal; meaning that there could have been 100 bands of

70 people, each led by one of the faithful prophets, who could have spread the good news of Baal's defeat and Yahweh's provision to all the people of Samaria. In the time of Jesus, *just one band* of 70 disciples spreading the good news through the villages of Samaria was enough to cause the satan to fall like lightning from heaven. Imagine the effect of 100 similar bands!

So based upon Jesus' 'commentary' on the acts of Elijah, I believe it's clear Elijah turned his back on his calling and, unlike Peter, did not turn back. God twice asks him at Horeb what he's doing there and twice receives the same answer—an answer that is full of distortion and inaccuracy. The best we can say for Elijah is that the spirit of forgetting and the spirit of panic gained such a foothold in his life that even when God sent fire, wind and earthquake they were not dislodged. And when they weren't evicted, God basically said to Elijah that he could retire—there were just three appointings and anointings that needed to be carried out first, none of which would require him to go anywhere near Jezebel. In fact, all of them could be done on the far side of the Jordan. He didn't need to have the slightest concern for his safety because God was looking out for him.

Now God's ideal plan for a parliament of prophets—wow! what a concept!—was no longer possible because of the time delay. But He still had Plan B for changing the government. Instead of the bands of 70 roaming believers, Elijah was tasked with anointing two new heads of state, Jehu and Hazael, as well as Elisha as a successor for himself. But Elijah baulked. For years. There were wars with Aram when various prophets—those whom Elijah claimed didn't exist—both advised and challenged Ahab over his conduct in various battles.

Then, after some time—indeterminate but clearly significant—the incident concerning Naboth's Vineyard occurred. Elijah himself went to confront Ahab over the murder of Naboth and his sons[50] and the dispossession of their family's inheritance. This meeting took place in the presence of Jehu. Eventually, an unknown amount of time later but following three years of peace with Aram, Ahab was killed in battle. Did Elijah take the opportunity then to seek out Jehu? No.

Ahab's son, Ahaziah, became king. His was a short reign, just two years. Still we're now talking, at minimum, nine years since Elijah was tasked with Plan B for governmental change. Perhaps it was as much as twice as long, maybe more.

And so on to Plan C. Was God thinking: 'If Elijah is too stubborn to do it, then the mandate for governmental change must fall to Elisha'? Certainly the timing was excellent. Ahaziah had just died around the same time as Elijah was taken up in a whirlwind. The briefness of Ahaziah's reign was, in my view, God's mercy. He was a follower of Beelzebub which, as pointed out in *Dealing with Belial*, is simply the spirit of abuse under another name. When a ruler is influenced by the spirit of armies, time and abuse, there's little hope for a nation.

Now when Elisha returned back across the Jordan, invested with a double portion of Elijah's spirit and carrying his mantle, did he fulfill Plan C by seeking out Jehu and Hazael?

Sigh. No.

Ahaziah's brother Joram came to the throne and reigned for twelve years.

We begin to see why Jesus had to come. These are the best of the best among the company of prophets. Their spectacular faith and crashing doubt, loyal obedience and treasonous delays, total fidelity and stark rebellion show forth a patchwork of blazing light and unutterable darkness. And they are like us. We are like them. We are complex mixtures of good and bad and, without the grace of God and the empowering work of Jesus, the rotting darkness in us will eventually triumph.

Elijah's complicity with Kronos caused him to be so dilatory about anointing Jehu and Hazael that he never did carry out these appointed tasks. He allowed Ahab and Jezebel, in their complicity with Belial—evidenced by the 'sons of Belial' Jezebel hired to falsely accuse Naboth of blasphemy—to perpetrate abuse for years longer than necessary. Elisha, too, was complicit with Kronos—for twelve years. By the time Jehu was finally anointed at least two decades had passed since Elijah had been at Horeb. Perhaps it was much longer.[51]

I cannot imagine that God did not place in Jehu's heart a sense of his calling to be king. Anyone who has ever felt called to accomplish a particular task but has had to wait for permission from a particular leader that turned out never to be forthcoming knows the grinding of hope as time goes by. There's that aching awareness of a vocation, an office or a position lost, along with a terrible wondering as to whether this is all deluded ambition. Ultimately, the passage of time becomes a test in its own right.

Jehu, for all his wild and callous brutality, remained loyal to a series of weak rulers, never seeking the throne until the moment he was anointed by one of the sons of the prophets. He'd waited two, maybe three decades, and when the moment finally arrived, nothing was going to stop him seizing the day. His authority was palpable—when messengers were sent to him, they simply fell into line at his command.

When we are complicit with the spirit of Time, it's all too easy for God's appointed times to be ignored, His seasons for change to be lost and the call on our lives to become untimely. Once Elijah had travelled down to Horeb, a journey of 46 days from Samaria, God's original plan for a prophetic company to bring change to the kingdom was no longer possible. By the time Elijah retraced his steps, the power vacuum would have been filled—as indeed it was, by the likes of Zedekiah, the prophet who went on to make iron horns and to be prepared to speak in the name of Yahweh, the God he did not serve.

Back in the days when the Israelites had just come out of Egypt, there was an appointed time for going up into the land. When ten of the twelve spies brought back a bad report, the people chose to follow them—until those ten spies died. The people then turned around, changed their minds and said they'd do as the Lord had commanded in the first place. Moses warned them, questioning their motives:

> *'Why are you now disobeying the Lord's orders to return to the wilderness? It won't work. Do not go up into the land now. You will only be crushed by your enemies because the Lord is not with you.'*
>
> Numbers 14:41–42 NLT

They ignored Moses, refused to believe it was too late and so got smashed in battle. It was 38 more years, while that entire generation died out, before their children could enter the land of promise.

When we're complicit with Kronos, we'll turn our backs on the appointed times of God, thinking that because He is Lord of Time, those 'kairos' moments are available whenever. But they are not, because we cannot have it both ways—we can't have a covenant with both Jesus and Belial.

> *What harmony is there between Christ and Belial?... As God has said... 'Come out from them and be separate.'*
>
> 2 Corinthians 6:15–17 NIV

This epistle was not written to unbelievers. If you think it is impossible for believers to have a covenant with Belial, then read Paul's words again. *Come out from them and be separate.* It's completely unnecessary to say this if complicity with Belial, agreements with Kronos, covenants with Death and pacts with Hell are not possible.

Come out from them and be separate through the grace of God and the atonement of Jesus.

What happened to Elijah that he simply couldn't obey God? At the end of the day, I suspect that his initial panic subsided into depression, and the depression slid into denial, and the denial got mired in shame. And every day, the shame rose just a little bit higher until it was an invincible mountain.

When we get stuck in shame, we're actually caught in a web of our own pride—pride that's been crushed but refuses to let go. Pride that finds self-exposure so unbearable it will go to extraordinary lengths to hide its flaws and faults.

Maybe as you've read these stories of Abraham and Elijah, Elisha and David, and realised that they aren't quite the heroes with haloes you've been taught, your self-esteem has upped a notch. Maybe you've thought, 'Good grief! They're as bad as I am!' or even 'For true and real? But I'm not as bad as that and I gotta tell ya, I'm rotten to the core!'

When self-esteem is all about comparison, it's a deadly treadmill. You've probably noticed I haven't been pandering to anyone's self-esteem with my relentless reminders about the only good Person in the universe. That's the only comparison worth anything and so it's a realistic assessment to confess we're corrupt right through. But that doesn't mean God doesn't value us and treasure us as His beloved; it doesn't mean He doesn't love us with a fierce I'll-die-for-you passion; it doesn't mean He doesn't have plans to turn our putrid muck into ravishing splendour.

Get over your complicity with shame—and therefore with pride, and with Leviathan, the spirit behind the sons of pride. God doesn't want to fix the pride behind our shame; He wants it nailed to the Cross and slain.

In the Garden Beyond Time, He accepted a cup full of our pride and shame, our complicity with abuse and with dishonour, our pacts with forgetting and wasting, and our covenantal agreements with Death, Hell, Time, War and others we don't even know the names of.

> *Jesus went out with His disciples beyond the winter stream of Kidron, where there was a garden.*
>
> John 18:1 BLB

Very few translations mention the 'winter-flowing' torrent, instead giving the impression that the water was a shallow, placid brook crossed with relative ease.

But the Kidron at night was then a black-shadowed valley with steep paths passing monuments and tombs cut into the rock. Its icy water was mixed with blood coming from effluent channels that dropped down from the Temple.

This was the time of Passover—the season of spring—but the winter-cold water, the darkness of the landscape with its rock-hewn tombs, and the blood in the stream are all evocative of the shadow of death, prefiguring what was soon to occur. The blood in the water foreshadowed the blood and water that would pour from the side of Jesus when, after His death, His body was pierced with a lance.

Wading through the blood of sacrifice in the Kidron water was a symbolic ratification of the new covenant just raised between Jesus and His disciples. For thousands of years people had solemnised the ancient ritual of blood covenant with a 'walk of blood'.

The timing of this crossing of the Kidron is reminiscent of the crossing of the Jordan as the Israelites were entering the land of promise. Both occurred just prior to Passover. Back in the days of Joshua, the Jordan was swollen with the winter thaw from the north. It was at flood stage when the waters stopped and rolled back to Adam.

As we've seen, the people of Israel were effectively asked to heal history, to take up where Adam had left off in his calling and become 'shomerim', *keepers and watchers who guard and steward a garden kingdom*. They were being asked to revisit a garden like unto Eden and to change the outcome. This is the constant call of God: to heal hearts and homes and history. All the miracles of Jesus where a particular location is specified have a healing-of-history aspect to them. All of them also have an edge-of-combat facet: Jesus was constantly at war with principalities and powers and world-rulers.

The crossing of the Kidron carried with it that same invitation to revisit the Garden—this time to the disciples. Yet not just to the disciples who were with Him at that moment, to all of us across all times. He asks us to become 'shomerim': *watchers* and *keepers*. He asks us to 'watch and pray'.

Just as the first Joshua crossed the Jordan, summoned to heal history through taking up stewardship of a new garden, so the second Joshua—Jesus—crossed the Kidron to a garden. Because of the blood coming from the Temple drains, it was a fertile place,[52] full of fruit trees and flowering shrubs. It would have been fragrant with blossom that evening on the cusp of the season of spring.

Anneli Sinkko, in pointing out the significance of the 'winter-flowing' torrent and the blood-infused water, connects Gethsemane to the Garden of Eden. Both are places of life, and of death. One is historical, she points out, and the other outside those bounds.

Secluded within the garden was an olive grove, Gethsemane, *the oil press*. Its name comes from Hebrew 'gath', *wine press*, and 'shemen', *oil*, which is also the word for *olive, fat* and *fertile*. While in the grove, Jesus fell into such deep anguish of soul that His sweat became like drops of blood. This pain and sweat are also evocative of Eden and the words of God:

> *I will sharply increase your pain...*
> *By the sweat of your brow you will eat your bread.*
>
> Genesis 3:16; 19 BSB

These words were spoken Adam and Eve, the 'shomerim' appointed by God—His regents of earth and its creatures, His keepers and guardians of the garden, His watchers and stewards. In asking His disciples to 'watch and pray', Jesus was appointing them as 'shomerim'.

But let's look at an even deeper parallel. Adam's first task as a regent was to *name*. He was given authority to speak out, to prophesy, to invoke and to declare the unique identity of both animals and humanity. When he handed his rights over to the serpent, that authority was lost—along with much else as well. Perhaps in fact it was a desire for this privilege of naming that was the motivation behind the plot to beguile Adam and Eve. Naming is an astounding authority, because a name is the ignition fuse for identity, destiny, calling, vocation, purpose, meaning. That God gave it to us and entrusted us with its power is stupefying.

Does the satan want it? As I said, I think his desire for it may well be a significant part of the motivation for the temptation in Eden. The satan was skilled in trading, and names were high on his profit list:

> *By the abundance of your trading you became filled with violence within, and you sinned; therefore I cast you as a profane thing out of the mountain of God; and I destroyed you, O covering cherub, from the midst of the fiery stones.*
>
> Ezekiel 28:16 NKJV

The word for *trading* in this statement of the expulsion of the satan from the garden on the mountain implies gossip, slander and libel: in effect, trading names and reputations, thus trading destinies and callings.

Part of a covenantal agreement is a trade. When we have a covenant with Kronos, we've traded away our future and receive the past in exchange. Why would we want our past back? Why would we want the trauma and pain to repeat itself? Why would we not appropriate what Jesus has already done on our behalf in upending the curse of Eden and allowing us access to His blessings over our callings?

The name Gethsemane contains the word 'shemen', *oil*. Yet it therefore also contains the word 'shem', *name*. I think this is important because in the grove of Gethsemane that Passover Eve, there were no olives being pressed. However, *name* and its associated destiny were under severe pressure. Jesus said,

> *Abba, Father, all things are possible to You; take away this cup from Me; but not what I will, but what You will.*
>
> Mark 14:36 BLB

The word for 'cup' was used symbolically to mean *lot* or *destiny*. Jesus was facing a test, as Adam had once faced a test. The first was about eating, the second about drinking. Both involved the destiny not just of themselves but of the entire world.

Like Eden lying in some liminal space that defies terrestrial geography and in a time that straddles both history and eternity, Gethsemane that night became the Garden Beyond Time. It was there that Jesus made the choice that He would reach out across time, through all the march of years, and accept onto Himself all of humanity's sin. He, the sinless One, decided to align Himself with the will of the Father. He would lay hold of sin from the beginning of days to their ending. It was as if He determined to corral not only sin but Time itself, plunging it into an eternal NOW and bounding it fast in a single hour.

He made the hour of His choice timeless, accessible to us through His sacrifice on the Cross. He wants us to retrieve our destiny from Belial and Kronos, because His was pressed to enable us to again become the 'shomerim' of the Lord: His stewards of the earth, His regents in our communities, His faithful watchers who ensure justice, His loving guardians of mercy, His garden-keepers who bring about the healing of history.

Prayer

Heavenly Father, it's me again, asking for help again.

Elijah went from the heights of assurance to the depths of depression. So did Simon Peter. On being sifted like wheat, winnowed to the point of overthrow, he crashed down in a heap. Both of them—Elijah and Peter—ran away to a place they felt safe, turning back to the old and familiar, hurrying back to what they used to be before You summoned them to follow You.

Lord, let me borrow from the words of the prophet Elijah who said, 'I am no better than my ancestors.' Well, Lord, I am no better than Elijah or Simon Peter and, though You want me to succeed where they failed, I desperately need Your help to avoid a fall into a depression that impacts me so badly I want to run from the calling You have placed on my heart.

Lord, when I step up to the threshold or to the threshing floor, I need so much more help than I can even begin to imagine. I'm facing tests that I've failed before and that my ancestors have failed before me and I don't know where I went wrong the first time. I made decisions that seemed right at the time but I look back now and wonder how I could ever have thought that.

Lord, in the Garden of Gethsemane, You asked Your friends to 'watch and pray'. I know You're asking me the same. That's the first port of call for Your help to come—to watch and pray. Yet, as You know, the spirit is willing but the flesh is weak. I need Your help even to ask for Your help. I need Your help for the strength to watch and pray.

Lord, as You provided a restorative breakfast for Elijah and for Simon Peter, please provide one for me. Grant me the strength and the sustenance to return, right at the critical moment. Renew my calling and, where my delays have caused others to miss the timing into their callings, I ask for Your reset of all that might be. I ask for Jesus, the redeemer of wasted time, to move us all back into alignment with Your plans and purposes. I ask for the appointed times to come again, so that we may respond to Your summons to us with refreshed vigour and new zeal. I even ask, as Mary did during the wedding at Cana, for You to find a way to bless Your people even when the timing is not quite right.

> And I ask this in the name of Jesus, the Lord and redeemer of time. Amen.

7

Timely and Untimely

WHEN WE RESIST GOD TOO LONG, more than our ability to enter our calling is compromised. We may deny others their calling because of our complicity with the enemies of God.

There have been several times in my life when I've been working as a volunteer with different organisations and felt called to take on a leadership role. It wasn't as if I really wanted to be a leader, given all of the responsibility and time-consuming management involved, it was the slow-dawning realisation I was saying *no* to God about stepping up to the position. I have to admit that I have a long track record of saying *no* to God that He has been extraordinarily gracious about. However, as it turned out, I was never offered any of those positions I felt called to. Not one of them.

When a sense of call deepens in strength over a decade and yet remains unfulfilled, tension builds in the soul. I began to wonder if I really heard from God, even as I prayed for the breakthroughs that never came. In the end, I concluded that I was wrong. Because, quite often over the years as I saw one person after another after another appointed to the role I felt called to, whatever private doubts I had about their capability soon vanished when they took up the position. They always turned out to be superb choices. I could see the hand of God on their lives.

It's only as I've been writing this book that I've come to reassess my conclusion. Maybe I was called, after all. I did eventually find out, a considerable time after I was no longer involved with one organisation, that I had several times been nominated for the role I felt God wanted me to fill. However, when my appointment was discussed, one leader put an end to it all with the question: 'Have you seen her house?'

It's the kind of random, stop-you-in-your-tracks question that you don't know what to do with and derails the discussion entirely. Apparently it was met with silence—a silence that was the end of any possibility my nomination would be approved.

Now my house was shabby and in need of repair. Unless something absolutely has to be fixed, it's still not a priority. A few decades ago I realised I had a choice: I could use any savings I accumulated to prettify my house or I could use them to do the things of God. My income wasn't sufficient to do both.

I chose not to focus on the upkeep of the house in order to pursue the calling of God. But my house became the excuse to deny the appointment to that calling. My choice became weaponised against me. My house, somehow, had become vastly more important than my character.

As I look at the story of Elijah, I ask myself: which of the threshold spirits was he in league with, that he denied Jehu and Hazael their calling for so long? That he even had doubts about God's call over the life of Elisha? When Elisha wants to say goodbye his parents, Elijah apparently has second thoughts:

> *'Go back again, for what have I done to you?'*
>
> 1 Kings 19:20 ESV

Yet Jesus would apparently have answered Elisha differently:

> *Another man said to Him, 'I am going to follow You, Lord, but first let me bid farewell to my people at home.'*
>
> *But Jesus told him, 'Anyone who puts his hand to the plough and then looks behind him is useless for the kingdom of God.'*
>
> Luke 9:61–62 PHPS

So which of the threshold spirits was Elijah complicit with? I can positively see six of the seven, so I have to assume all of them. Python the constrictor, Ziz the shredder of truth, Leviathan the retaliator, Rachab the waster, Azazel the inducer of panic, Belial-Kronos the abuser—they are easy enough to see. Lilith—no, not so apparent. But then she rarely is.

What do we do when we realise that a person or group is so completely in thrall to the entire cabal of threshold guardians they are blocking access to our calling? What do we do when we sense the veto will go on indefinitely? Do we wait and serve like Jehu, for as long as it takes? Or do we decide enough time has gone by and try to kick open the door ourselves? Or do we leave and invest our talents elsewhere?

This is such a hard decision. We have to do what God tells us. And that may change as we follow Him from one season to another.

When we're faced with a sense of calling that is stifled over a long period of time, we're being opposed by an individual or system completely complicit with Belial-Kronos. Now by 'long period', I don't mean several weeks or even months. That might simply be a test we have to pass so that patience, as a Fruit of the Spirit, is ripened to maturity within us. By 'long period', I mean a calling that endures over several years but is smothered, despite repeated opportunity for advancement. I mean the Elijah-and-Jehu scenario: the leader is aware the call is divine, and has the opportunity to make the appointment, but withholds it indefinitely.

Such an Elijah-like leader has condemned God's choice—has overridden the plans and purposes of God and judged them to be *worthless*. Such leaders decide they know better than God, exactly as Belial did. The Watchers were aware of God's intentions for the redemption of humanity and tried to thwart them. When leaders are complicit with Belial, they duplicate that ancient conspiracy on a micro-level—and try to frustrate God's plans for some individuals under their leadership.

In addition, because the alter-ego of Belial is Kronos, they spin out the time as far as possible towards complete wasting of calling. The leaders protect themselves from criticism by making use of the maturing Fruit of 'chesed'—faithfulness, goodness and kindness—in God's chosen appointees. Any lapse proves their point: the ones God has called are not yet ready for promotion.

Now in condemning God's choices, such leaders thereby condemn the ones called and also condemn the decision-making choices they've made to reach that point. In denying them an appointment to their calling, the leader is sacrificing to Belial the destiny of others—not to mention their identity and soul. This means they've invalidated any sacrifices the ones called have made in pursuit of God's purpose for their lives.

This is why my house was the specific reason given as to why I couldn't enter my calling: because it's a *legal* sacrifice that had to be delegitimised. Our *specific* choices are targeted.

At thresholds, the spirit guardians will ask us for a sacrifice. That's part of their testing regime. And normally, people offer one of three:

- we sacrifice others or our relationship with them
- we sacrifice ourselves
- we sacrifice the honour of God.

None of these are legal offerings because they deny the atonement. As I've explained about these sacrifices in *God's Priority*,[53] they are denials of the all-sufficiency of the atonement of Jesus. We are effectively saying to Jesus: 'What You did on the cross is enough for my salvation but it isn't enough to allow me to access my calling.'

That is not to say a sacrifice is unnecessary. But the sacrifice must be to, and for, God—not to appease any threshold guardian. We are called to *make* a sacrifice, not *be* a sacrifice. Anything that crosses the line into *being* a sacrifice is forbidden by God. That's the whole point of the story of Isaac at Moriah.

But aren't we called to be 'living sacrifices'? After all, Paul says:

> *Therefore, I urge you, brothers and sisters, in view of God's mercy, to offer your bodies as a living sacrifice, holy and pleasing to God—this is your true and proper worship.*
>
> Romans 12:1 NIV

The opening word, 'therefore', connects this to his long previous discussion—three chapters long—about the Gentiles entering God's kingdom before the Jewish people. But don't become conceited as a result, Paul advises—instead be holy and pleasing to God. The call to *be* a living sacrifice is not about becoming an offering to placate or appease God or present Him with an acceptable inducement for entry to our calling. All of that is a subtle denial of the atonement. The call to *be* a living sacrifice is to present ourselves for transformation so we can align ourselves with God's will, as the very next verse testifies:

> *Do not conform to the pattern of this world, but be transformed by the renewing of your mind. Then you will be able to test and approve what God's will is—His good, pleasing and perfect will.*
>
> Romans 12:2 NIV

Paul's talking about a gift, not a bribe. Ultimately there are legal and illegal sacrifices. Illegal sacrifices are fundamentally bribes to the threshold guardians. Legal sacrifices are gifts to God, not to the threshold spirits, gifts made without any acquisitive eye towards God's rewards.

Yet it's possible for legal choices and sacrifices, particularly in priorities of time and money, that we've made in the past to be flipped right over and back against us. Those choices and sacrifices are transmuted through some alchemy of inversion so that we ourselves become the chosen sacrifice.

Quite often we're not even aware we've been made over into the sacrifice to Belial-Kronos. We have the sense of calling but we don't know God's appointed time, so we watch and pray. Once we become aware that our calling is passing from timely to untimely and we've become someone else's sacrifice, we cannot stay in the situation.

We either push for the door to open to our calling—and possibly get expelled in the process—or we leave.

We cannot allow ourselves to be sacrificed to Belial. We cannot allow the sacrifices we have offered to God to be appropriated and converted into sacrifices to Kronos. Otherwise we become complicit with the engineering of our own destruction—we've begun to resource the war against ourselves.

So we have to discern this situation for what it is, judge accurately—yes, *judge*, but *not* condemn as we have been condemned. Unless we forgive, we repeat the toxic cycle of collusion with Belial and Kronos. We may also need to repent of allowing a leader to confiscate our gifts to God and instead dedicate them to the spirit of abuse. Because, although we may not have had any part in it or even any knowledge of the seizure, nevertheless it still happened on our watch.

Once we become complicit with Kronos, timely becomes untimely. Elijah, and to a lesser extent Elisha, were responsible for the decades-long delay in the anointing of Jehu. Elijah's deferral eventually led to the untimely death of Naboth and his sons when Ahab took a liking to their inheritance and Jezebel partnered with some sons of Belial to get it for her husband.

It's easy to spout the cliché: God's in control. God's on His throne. God's in charge. God reigns in heaven.

But that all too often fails to acknowledge: 'It's complicated.'

Yes, God's still in control, still on the throne, still in charge, still reigning in heaven—*but* His will is not being done on earth. Ultimately, yes it will be. Because it doesn't matter how wrong something goes, He can still work it out for our good. However He will never violate our free will, He will never coercively control us. That would be abuse. He does not impose a fate upon us, He summons us to a destiny. Yet we can refuse that destiny, as Jonah did.

In some Jewish translations of 2 Kings 9, where the story of the anointing of Jehu is recounted, the 'young man from the company of the prophets' who is sent by Elisha and entrusted with this task of king-making is identified as Jonah. This was, of course, in his earlier days before he was sent to Nineveh.[54]

Now isn't this possibility an intriguing thought? We readily pick up on Jonah's reluctance to obey the will of God and preach to the people of Nineveh. After all, he does a runner and takes a ship heading for the far side of the then-known world. Yet we don't see the possibility that, if those Jewish commentators are right, then he's the third generation of prophet to tell God He was making the wrong decision and that His choices were wrong. We eventually find out it wasn't fear of the people of Nineveh that prompted Jonah's defiance, it was anger at the possibility God was about to extend mercy to the Assyrians—those pitiless people who, according to Nahum, were counselled by Belial.

Our resistance to God, when it is pre-meditated and persistent, is of course the very opposite of faithfulness. It's the complete reverse of 'chesed'. It draws Belial into our lives. The famous prophecy concerning the coming of Immanuel is also a declaration of the coming of the Assyrians, those Belial-advised persecutors:

> *The Lord said to Isaiah, 'Go out, you and your son Shear-Jashub, to meet Ahaz at the end of the aqueduct of the Upper Pool, on the road to the Launderer's Field. Say to him, "Be careful, keep calm and don't be afraid. Do not lose heart..."'*
>
> *Again the Lord spoke to Ahaz, 'Ask the Lord your God for a sign, whether in the deepest depths or in the highest heights.'*
>
> *But Ahaz said, 'I will not ask; I will not put the Lord to the test.'*
>
> *Then Isaiah said, 'Hear now, you house of David! Is it not enough to try the patience of humans? Will you try the patience of my God also? Therefore the Lord himself will give you a sign: The virgin will conceive and give birth to a son, and will call him Immanuel. He will be eating curds and honey when he knows enough to reject the wrong and choose the right, for before the boy knows enough to reject the wrong and choose the right, the land of the two kings you dread will be laid waste.*
>
> *The Lord will bring on you and on your people and on the house of your father a time unlike any*

*since the day Ephraim separated from Judah—
He will bring the king of Assyria.'*

Isaiah 7:3-4;10-17 NIV

Ahaz was afraid of invasion by two northern kings. Isaiah tried to encourage him and delivered a message *'at the end of the aqueduct of the Upper Pool, on the road to the Launderer's Field.'* It's no coincidence that, in this very same spot, a generation later, the Assyrians delivered their ultimatum to the officials of King Hezekiah. This is a place where Belial obviously had legal rights because of the refusal of Ahaz to even ask God for a sign.

There is no question that Ahaz had a covenant with Belial.

Ahaz... cast metal images of Baal, burned incense in the Ben-hinnom Valley, and burned his sons as an offering, following the detestable activities of the nations whom the Lord had expelled in front of the people of Israel. He sacrificed and burned incense on high places, on the top of hills, and under every green tree.

2 Chronicles 28:1-4 ISV

Ahaz sacrificed his sons. He sacrificed his future. It's thought that one of the sons was actually Immanuel. That untimely death would explain why Isaiah's prophecy didn't appear to come true: like those leaders who know the calling of God rests on a person but resist appointing them to it, thus sacrificing their destiny, so too Ahaz had been told the calling of God on his children and yet he sacrificed them to try to buy immunity from the dark powers of the spirit world.

The protection Ahaz sought was useless. Because he chose to defy the prophecy, he was invaded by those he feared. Jesus used what happened next in one of His most famous parables:

As a result, the Lord his God handed Ahaz over to the king of Aram, who defeated him and took a large number of captives away to Damascus. Ahaz was also delivered over to the control of the King of Israel, who defeated him with many heavy casualties... carried away 200,000 women, sons, and daughters... took a great deal of plunder, and brought it all to Samaria.

But a prophet of the Lord was there named Oded. He went out to greet the army as it arrived in Samaria. He warned them, 'Look! Because the Lord God of your ancestors was angry at Judah, He delivered them into your control, but you have killed them with a vehemence that has reached all the way to heaven! Now you're intending to make the men and women of Judah and Jerusalem to be your slaves. Surely you have your own sins against the Lord your God for which you're accountable, don't you? So listen to me! Return the captives whom you've captured from your brothers, because the anger of the Lord is burning hot against you!'

Some of the leaders... of Ephraim... stood up to the army as they were coming back from the battle and told them, 'Don't bring those captives here! You'll bring even more guilt on us from the Lord, in addition to our own existing sin and guilt! He's already mad enough against Israel because of our guilt!'

So the army abandoned the captives and the war booty in front of the officers and the entire assembled retinue. After this, some men who were chosen by name took charge of the captives, clothed those who were naked with clothes appropriated from the war booty, gave them clothes and sandals, fed them, gave them something to drink, anointed them with oil, provided those who weren't able to walk with donkeys to ride on, and took them back to their relatives at Jericho, the city of palm trees.

Then they returned to Samaria.

2 Chronicles 28:5–15 ISV

In the light of the backstory here, Jesus' answer to the question, 'Who is my neighbour?' has deep historical and political overtones involving the guilt of leaders and their dismissal of God's will.

Our choices have ramifications, generation upon generation. We will reap what we sow. If we deny someone an advancement into a new aspect of their calling, we will eventually be denied the same and so will our children and grandchildren. Untimely death is a consequence of worshipping Belial. And this not simply in the style of Ahaz sacrificing his sons. There's also the curse on the descendants of the high priest Eli to be considered: when blindness and untimely death was the end result of Eli honouring his sons more than he honoured God. His tolerance of the physical, sexual and spiritual abuse perpetrated by his children, actually named as 'sons of Belial', became a death sentence in succeeding generations.

And yet we see it's possible to overturn such ruinous complicity with this spirit that's so hostile it doesn't simply want us destroyed, it wants us to devise our own destruction and that of our children. We have to acknowledge that such overturning is rare. It's as rare as the Samaritans in the time of Ahaz who called out their countrymen for abusing and enslaving their neighbours the Judeans; it's as rare as the people of Nineveh repenting at the preaching of Jonah; it's as rare as the surviving son of Ahaz, King Hezekiah, turning away from the covenant with Death and all the false refuges associated with it and receiving a miracle so stupendous that Time went backwards.

This is the call upon us. To renounce our covenants with Kronos-Belial, whether they have been of our own making, whether they have come unrevoked down our generational line, whether we have had them imposed on us by leaders who, unauthorised, reformulated our sacrifices to God into offerings to the spirit of Time and abuse. It doesn't matter whether we are innocent or guilty, we need to end the alliance. The only way we can safely do that is put the annulment proceedings entirely in the hands of Jesus. To ask Him to finalise it through the power of His blood, shed on our behalf.

But I believe our choices need cleansing too. After realising that my choices involving my house had been defiled, I spoke to my house and told it that those words spoken over it were unauthorised. That Belial had no place in the choices involving it. If the walls can talk to the rafters, as it says in Habukkuk, then they can hear me. And I didn't want there to be any possibility that it could be said in the spirit realm or anywhere else:

> *You have devised shame for your house... the stone will cry out from the wall, and the beam from the woodwork respond.*
>
> Habukkuk 2:10–11 ESV

I want my house to be a blessing, even beyond my own time.

Amongst the angels listed in the Book of 1 Enoch is a spirit called Kasyade, fifth-ranking amongst the leaders of the Watcher rebellion.[55] The name means the *covering hand* and is derived from 'kesed', *Chaldean* or *Babylonian* or *astrologer*. Sometimes 'kesed' is spelled 'chesed', thus reminding us of the *lovingkindness* of God.

The *covering hand* is meant to evoke overshadowing protection like the shielding Cloud of Glory. However Kasdaye, on leaving her first estate, began to teach exactly the opposite of protection. She instructed humanity in the art of assault—the striking of an embryo to bring about an abortion, the striking of serpents causing snakebite, the striking of the sun in heatstroke.[56] Instead of the weaponised Fruit 'chesed', *goodness, kindness, faithfulness*—weapons of healing instead of harm—these are missiles of destruction. As usual, God's gifts to us are perverted in the hands of Belial and his allies.

The natural alliance between Kasyade the womb-striker and Kronos the child-eater, together with the mind control of Belial, affects our society's attitude towards children so deeply that they have long been seen as a commodity. Child abuse is not new. It was there when indigenous children were abducted from their parents; it was there when children were bundled off as farm workers to Canada and Australia while their mothers were in British hospitals giving birth to a younger child; it was there during the sexual molestation of youngsters in schools, churches, orphanages and institutions as well as the subsequent cover-ups; it was there in the eugenics experimentation on children during the last century and their renewal in this century; it was there in countless violations of medical ethics when children are injected with substances that doctors themselves will not administer to their own children or grandchildren; it was there in abortion up to birth and it's there, now, when some activists call for 'abortion' up to one year of age. That used to be called infanticide.

By the early second century, Christians routinely risked their lives to save unwanted children. They went out at night to find newborns left to die by exposure or by wild animals hunting. Such rescue missions brought them into conflict with those engaged in the sex trade and slavery. The *Didache*, a Christian text from this time, said: 'Do not murder a child by abortion, nor kill it at birth.' The epistle of Barnabas from a few decades later confirms: 'Do not murder a child by abortion, nor again, destroy that which is born.'

Today Christians are no longer united on this issue. Belial has managed to convince us to dehumanise and devalue unborn children and classify them as blobs or cell-clumps! These terms are used to deny that a child in the womb is an image-bearer of God, and so deprive them of any legal recognition as persons until they are born. And now the first flags are being waved, signalling a move to delay that recognition until a full year after birth.

Yet John the Baptist leaped for joy in his mother's womb when Mary came to visit her cousin Elizabeth. At six months in utero, John was excited to know Jesus was physically nearby! He reacted with real emotion to the presence of God.

Since ancient times, abortions have been used as a form of contraception. Herbal medicines, sharp tools with force and other traditional methods were common. Although abortion laws naturally differ throughout the world because of cultural or religious views, wealthier nations have instigated increasingly coercive control of their poorer neighbours by tying the flow of economic aid to enacting liberal abortion laws.

Frank Pavone states, 'A discussion of abortion, whether private or public, should acknowledge the pain that most of us feel about it, whether we describe ourselves as pro-life or not. The psychological attitude to take and to convey is, "You are not my enemy. We are in this painful situation together and need to help each other out of it." We should deal with the individual who may react angrily to the mention of abortion much as we would to a person who is afflicted by personal disasters. These are not enemies. These are people in pain.'

We only ever see a tiny sliver of people's lives. Only Jesus sees and knows the hurts and wounds and depths of each life. We are never able to see anyone's entire journey or where they are in their walk of faith. As the Greek philosopher Plato said, 'Be kind, for everyone you meet is fighting a hard battle.'

I would add: don't just be kind, be good and faithful too. Let a torrent of God's 'chesed' flow through you. The enemy is never another person: it is the spirit of abuse. And that spirit has groomed a child of God through several generations to choose death, rather than life— and to believe exactly the opposite is being chosen.

By having an abortion, a woman is unwittingly terminating her own destiny, her own future. She's not gaining, she's losing. In addition, her family has also lost a part of its destiny. The spirit of abuse has stolen it, all the while insisting that this works for our benefit, not our detriment.

Mother Teresa said, 'Abortion kills twice. It kills the body of the baby and the conscience of the mother. Three-quarters of its victims are women: half the babies and all the mothers.'

Shame, guilt and self-rejection are frequent visitors who come to oppress our personal spirits. They add a sense of failure and unworthiness, and lead to a powerlessness in stepping across the threshold into our destiny. A sacrifice of a child at the instigation of Belial-Kronos-Moloch is a powerful covenantal offering. Once we have offered part of the destiny of our family, it's not such a hard decision next time to offer more—to offer the rest of our identity, our destiny, our calling.

The spirit of abuse will always oppress the child who survives an abortion attempt. Kronos and Kasyade may even pretend to be protectors. I know of a survivor who has seen the image of the covering hand and thought it was Jesus. It's all about deception—attempting to draw even survivors of failed abortions into alliances that would normally be unthinkable for them. This spirit of abuse attaches itself to trauma, moving down generational lines and blighting the future. A lack of compassion towards children is a symptom of affliction by this accuser of the saints.

It's no coincidence that lack of compassion is associated with abortion. In the Hebrew language, compassion is derived from the word for *womb*—it's a love so intense it doesn't come from the brain or the heart but from the space deep within where we are meant to be enfolded and cherished. If the womb becomes a place of death, then it cannot give birth to compassion.

In the Greek language, on the other hand, compassion is connected to the *gut*. As indicated in *Dealing with Belial*, the gut is a critical repository of emotional memory. It keeps the files on which organs have lodged the memories of trauma experiences. The belly is the storehouse that needs to give access to the Living Water of Jesus for healing to occur. So often victims are unable to drink deeply of the Living Water because they are trying to pour into the wrong place: the brain rather than the gut.

'We could end this whole situation if you'd just jump,' Charlie Chaplain callously said to his 16-year-old pregnant bride, Lita Grey, while they were waiting for the train on the way back from their wedding ceremony in Mexico. They'd been together for three years.

The spirit of abuse and of abortion, is callous, not compassionate. When we are complicit with it or victimised by it, we can neither adequately give compassion, nor receive it. This may even be true when we are a survivor of a failed abortion attempt, or because abortion has been a systemic part of the lives of women in our generational stream.

Compassion is a complete contrast to abuse. But because we can't talk about abortion, we can't receive compassion. That suits Belial just fine. Brian E. Fisher writes: 'Abortion has entered the cultural realm of "religion" and "politics"—subjects we don't talk about in the company of family, co-workers and strangers. It's too awkward, too personal, too heavy, and will likely invite conflict we want to avoid.'

How sad this is for those who want to process their experience and heal.

An unborn child of eight week's gestation recoils from pain, has fingerprints, along with all major organs functioning. The baby can feel the mother's emotions and hear all that goes on outside the abdomen as if it's a drum.

Cassy Fiano says, 'It's almost conclusively provable that preborn babies can feel pain at 20 weeks gestation, although they respond to touch as early as eight weeks. There is also increasing evidence that preborn babies can feel pain much earlier than 20 weeks—possibly as early as five weeks. Some evidence exists to show that fetal pain may be even worse in the first trimester, "due to the uneven maturation of fetal neurophysiology."'[57]

Mother Teresa has pointed out: 'Any country that accepts abortion is not teaching its people to love, but to use any violence to get what they want. This is why the greatest destroyer of love and peace is abortion.'

We have become corporately and governmentally desensitised these last fifty years. Surgical abortion is effected by forced expulsion, suction, surgery or saline solution which causes burning. Late-term or full-term abortion involves the brain being sucked out of the live baby, which then may perhaps be harvested for body parts to be sold. Our hearts are calloused and hardened with and by technology and the impact of constant media acceptance.

Yet this is not a fight against flesh and blood but against the dark rulers and powers in heavenly places. And because it is not a fight against flesh and blood, we must always remember the enemy is not men and women—they are all victims in differing ways.

God calls us to have compassion for everyone, even those with whom we categorically disagree. Let us turn to Him and ask for a rain of His mercy. Our society has moved so perilously close to the attitudes of ancient Rome where a citizen could write to his wife: 'I beg and plead with you to take care of our little child, and as soon as we receive wages, I will send them to you. In the meantime, if (good fortune to you!) you give birth, if it is a boy, let it live; if it is a girl, expose it.'

We need transformation to see the unborn as sacred and to provide support and ongoing care to expectant mothers who are fearful of the future. But in trying to save their future, they are actually sacrificing it. The spirit of abuse always targets the most vulnerable—all too often children who are helpless and defenceless. The unborn are even more so because they are voiceless. In silencing them forever, the enemy of our souls has ferociously devoured more than life—he's demolished the destiny of individuals, families, communities and nations.

Isaiah 55 begins with an invitation to heal the loss of destiny as well as the trauma of abuse and abortion through drinking the Living Water of the Lord:

> *Come, everyone who thirsts, come to the waters;*
> *and he who has no money, come, buy and eat!*
> *Come, buy wine and milk without money and without price.*

Isaiah 55:1 ESV

The Living Water is priceless. No one will ever have enough money to purchase it. And yet, Isaiah goes on, God encourages us to buy it simply by turning to Him. He offers it as a grace-gift to us if we call out to Him and return to Him.

> *Turn to the Lord! He can still be found.*
> *Call out to God! He is near.*
> *Give up your evil ways and your evil thoughts.*
> *Return to the Lord our God. He will be merciful and forgive your sins.*

Isaiah 55:6–7 ESV

The Living Water of the Holy Spirit that rivers out from the belly of the Holy One is the perfect balm to heal the emotional memory that is filed away in our own bellies. We are able to draw on the Water through the Holy Spirit and, by it, God promises to wipe away every tear, to heal every painful remembrance, and to bring the ravages of Time to an end.

> *'Behold, the dwelling place of God is with man, and He will dwell with them. They will be His*

> *people, and God Himself will be with them as their God. He will wipe away every tear from their eyes, and there will be no more death or mourning or crying or pain, for the former things have passed away.'*
>
> *And the One seated on the throne said, 'Behold, I make all things new.'*

Revelation 21:3–5 BSB

This is His pledge to us: to make all things new. To redeem our choices, to redeem our wasted time, to redeem our lives, to redeem the past itself so that our inheritance in Him is secure.

When I was a kid, I would often think to myself that I didn't like the ending of a television episode I'd just watched and I'd go to bed restructuring the storyline in my mind. I'd try to analyse where the plot started going wrong and, from there, I'd devise a new finale. Sometimes this took days before I found a way to bring about a satisfactory resolution.

It never occurred to me until very recently that God does just this. Jesus remakes the endings of stories. In His life, it's possible to see the beginnings of re-enactments of historical events, before the changepoint is unveiled, and a critical departure from the old storyline changes the ending. These are lovely, lovely, lovely, happily-ever-after wondrous wrap-ups—Emmaus and Sychar, the journey from Bethany-beyond-the-Jordan to Bethany near Jerusalem, the double healing at Jericho. Each of these events reaches deep into the past to heal history and redeem time.[58]

If I were to ask which of the prophets defied God, most people with some biblical knowledge would automatically answer 'Jonah'. But, as we've seen, Jewish tradition names him as the young man who anointed Jehu. And that would mean that he had some extremely good role models in Elijah and Elisha when it came to not doing as God had asked.

Now, I actually think this Jewish tradition is correct. I have a secret method for assessing the accuracy of stories alleged to be Jewish folklore. Allow me to let you in on it. I simply look for the answer to this question: does this story play out in the life of Jesus? And if the answer is *yes*, then I'm prepared to believe the story is true.

So let's refresh our minds about Elijah's story, so we can discover the critical moment of choice that leads to a life that ultimately doesn't end well. It's when Elijah is running from Jezebel and sits down under the broom tree out from Beersheba. An angel cooks him a breakfast of bread on hot coals and, in the strength of that food, he travels for forty days to Mount Horeb where He hears the still, small voice of God and is commissioned to anoint Jehu, Hazael and Elisha. That food was not provision to go on, it was to sustain him on the way back to Samaria where he was supposed to form bands of seventy believers—just as Jesus did in a later age—to bring the people back to God.

The next time we see a breakfast of bread baked on hot coals in Scripture, it also includes fish, and it happens by the Sea of Galilee after the resurrection. Simon Peter has just thrown over his calling and decided to go back to his old profession as a fisherman. Jesus recalls him and restores him. But look at how Jesus three times addresses him: Simon, son of Jonah. Not Peter, not Cephas, but son of *Jonah*.

Elijah's mantle that was passed to Elisha and then to Jonah, then to Jonah's namesake John the Baptist, then to Jesus is, in this scene, being passed to Simon.[59] Many commentators are of the view that the apostle John finishes his gospel with the not-so-subtle message: 'Peter was a screw-up, but I'm the one with the halo. I'm the beloved disciple.'

No. Just no.

There are many deeply hidden allusions to Elijah here—while they are extremely overt in the matching chiasmus at the beginning of the gospel. The comments about 'taking off clothes' and 'dressing' are meant to draw our attention to what's happening: the passing of the mantle. Clearly some believers in the early Christian community thought the apostle John had inherited Elijah's mantle and would be, like Elijah, deathless. However in this scene, he specifically denies this and informs his readers that Jesus did not say he wouldn't die.

Simon, son of *Jonah*.

Now, let's move on from the critical moment of choice in Elijah's story to look at a similar crunch-point for the prophet Jonah. It's when he boards a ship for Tarshish. Where did he do this? Joppa. Why did he do it? Because he was the only prophet called to speak directly to the Gentiles, because he didn't want to go, and also because he didn't want God to show mercy to the very people who would oppress his countrymen.

Over half a millennia later, Simon son of Jonah also went to Joppa. He was staying by the sea. There, he fell into a trance and three times he received the same vision from God—a sail full of unclean creatures. *'Do not call anything impure that God has made clean,'*[60] a voice told him. While he was trying to work out the meaning of the vision, a delegation of Gentiles arrived at the gate asking for him.

Here's the critical moment of choice. Would Peter 'do a Jonah' and refuse to extend God's mercy to the Gentiles? After all, these were not just any Gentiles—they were Romans, the very people who were then oppressing his countrymen. Worse still, the delegation represented a centurion.

Yet perhaps Peter called to mind that moment when Jesus commended another centurion with the words, *'Truly I tell you, I have not found anyone in Israel with such great faith.'*[61]

He went with the delegation to meet the centurion Cornelius—and so, by God's grace and with controversy, the incoming of the Gentiles began.

Every follower of Jesus is called to heal history, to change the outcome of past tragedies. As Jesus summons the past to account, He stands with us, empowering our calls for the rolling back of Time so He can redeem the brokenness.

There are mantles and inheritances meant to pass through His hands so they can be cleansed before being restored to us. Let us not waste another moment in delay. Let us heed His call to the Garden or to the Lakeside and let us commune with Immanuel, God with us, in that eternal NOW that is beyond time.

Prayer

Heavenly Father,

There's an old, old story—a tragedy—that You want me to rewrite. I don't know what it's about, but inadequate as I am, I'm still the perfect person to change the ending. You've chosen me for reasons that are part of who I am, my family ancestry, my nationality, my cultural heritage, but the events of the past are so sanitised to make the victors look good that Your purposes are mostly or completely hidden from me.

Maybe, like Simon son of Jonah, I've got the right family name or connections. Maybe like Simon visiting Joppa, I'm at the right location. Maybe like Simon from Galilee, I've got the right ethnic background. Maybe like Simon the fisherman, I've got the right job. Maybe it's all of those things, maybe just one of them.

Maybe I'm reluctant. Maybe I've got prejudice and uncertainty to overcome. Maybe I'm just confused. Actually, Lord, mostly I'm confused. You could ask me to partner with You to heal history and it would just be so strange, I'd mess it up because I'd rely too much on my rational senses than on Your leading.

At any critical moment of choice, when the changepoint in the old, old story arrives and You want me to be a part of writing a new ending, help me to know Your will. In Your mercy, be as clear to me as You were to Peter with that vision of a sail that dropped down from heaven.

Lord, there are appointed times and seasons in each person's life. I've missed many of them. Some because I was complicit with Kronos and delayed too long or acted too hastily. Some because I sacrificed to a threshold guardian and sabotaged my calling. Some because I feared the unknown. I didn't want to stand in Your Council and plead for more time for my nation or my community. I was like Jonah, I wanted to see Your justice enacted, not Your mercy. But sometimes I wanted the opposite—like Abraham entreating for the people of Sodom, I wanted to see Your mercy prevail, not Your justice.

Help me to know Your times and timing.

> *There is a season (a time appointed) for everything and a time for every delight and event or purpose under heaven—*
> *A time to be born and a time to die;*
> *A time to plant and a time to uproot what is planted.*
> *A time to kill and a time to heal;*
> *A time to tear down and a time to build up.*
> *A time to weep and a time to laugh;*
> *A time to mourn and a time to dance.*
> *A time to throw away stones and a time to gather stones;*

A time to embrace and a time to refrain from embracing.
A time to search and a time to give up as lost;
A time to keep and a time to throw away.
A time to tear apart and a time to sew together;
A time to keep silent and a time to speak.
A time to love and a time to hate;
A time for war and a time for peace.

Ecclesiastes 3:1–8 AMP

May I be so in tune with the rhythm of Your heart, Father, that I never miss these times.

In Jesus' name. Amen.

Appendix 1
Summary

THE GOVERNMENT OF HEAVEN is ordered through the Divine Council, an administrative body in which God consults with His creation. Glimpses are given into the activity of the Divine Council in Psalm 82, Psalm 89, Job 1, 1 Kings 22, Isaiah 6, Jeremiah 23.

The Hebrew word 'elohim' is variously translated in the Bible as *God, gods, goddesses, judges, rulers, divine beings*. Michael Heiser suggests its original meaning was *'inhabitants of the heavenly realm'* which includes God but is not restricted to Him.

The name 'Yahweh' is not ambiguous but the plural word 'elohim' is. Translators generally decide by the context whether 'elohim' means *God* or *angelic rulers*. The distinctive phrase 'ha'elohim' means *the elohim* and, despite its general translation as *God*, it is proposed here that it is meant to be a clear indicator towards *angels*. The first appearance of 'ha'elohim' occurs in relation to Enoch who, according to the Book of Enoch, journeyed with angels much more than conversing with God. Thus Enoch's walk with 'ha'elohim' is not unambiguously with God, but could be with the angels.

Abraham is tested by 'ha'elohim' when he is asked to offer Isaac. Yahweh stops the test. This suggests that 'ha'elohim' may be fallen threshold guardians, not Yahweh; and this would be in keeping with the role of the threshold guardians and also with the words of the apostle James who says that God does not tempt/test anyone.

The spirit of abuse, Belial, has an alter-ego in Kronos, the spirit of Time. The original description of Kronos as serpentine with three heads—a man, a bull and a lion—seems to combine the attributes of a fiery snake-like seraph and the four-faced cherubim—with their man, ox, lion and eagle aspects.

Belial is one of the names given for the leader of the Watchers who descended to the earth, taking oaths to mate with human women. According to Peter in his epistle, the Watchers were eventually incarcerated in Tartarus, the netherhell, the lowest dungeon in the underworld. In Greek mythology Kronos, the titan who ate his own children, was imprisoned in Tartarus.

The Watchers who left heaven—and not all of them did—became the fathers of the *nephilim*, the giants. The *nephilim* in turn fathered the *gibborim*, the mighty men of old. Both *nephilim* and *gibborim* were drowned in the Great Flood, but their spirits survived to become demons—*shedim*, goat demons, or *rephaim*, ghosts of the warrior dead. God forbade His people to have anything to do with the worship of these entities—in fact, to destroy any city and its people who did so and leave their land desolate forever.

The Watchers are not the same as principalities. After the dispersal of the population following the Tower of Babel, God appointed seventy angels to watch over and shepherd the nations. Eventually these cosmic princes also became corrupt and they are, perhaps, the source of the giant clans who appeared occasionally after the Flood.

God meantime reserved Israel to Himself and began the building of His human family by calling Abraham into covenant with Him. Abraham however was an enabler of his wife Sarah when it came to abuse of her servant Hagar who was also his second wife. Because the principle of sowing-and-reaping is built into the fabric of the universe, his descendants suffered slavery and abuse. In addition, his failure to repent gave legal rights to the spirit of abuse to test him. Words that connect back to Hagar's experience during the binding of Isaac at Mount Moriah suggest the outworking of abuse. In a later era, the extremely similar experience of David at exactly the same spot—after he has become complicit with the spirit of armies, and thus the spirit of abuse—suggest that Abraham's test was not instigated by Yahweh but brought to an end by Him. The ram as a symbol of Hammon, another name for Kronos, and the possibility that the thicket was surrounding a threshing floor, suggest Abraham may have travelled to a known place of divination.

Moriah may always have been a threshing floor, not just in David's time. This would explain why Isaiah prophesies a new cornerstone for Zion—the original was defiled. Isaiah 28 not only prophesies a new cornerstone but outlines the requirements for God to show Himself strong as Lord of Time—similar to the day when Joshua called for the sun and the moon to stand still. There's not just a need for a precious, undefiled Cornerstone but also for a Cloud of glory. No false refuges, no ungodly covenants—get these things lined up and God is willing to send in angel armies to your defence and to give you more time to defeat your enemies. This is what Isaiah prophesied and also what, incredibly, came to pass when Hezekiah asked for the shadow on the steps to move backward.

There are other symbols of time resetting in Scripture: the rolling back of the Sea when the Israelites were fleeing Egypt has a sense of the pulling back of a Day. So too does the crossing of the Jordan when the waters were heaped up at Adam—as if calling the people back to the Garden. The olive press of Gethsemane, the secluded garden in the Kidron Valley, with its covenantal imagery of the 'walk of blood', is another place where time is paused. It was there that Jesus called His disciples, and us, to 'watch and pray', to return to the task of the *shomerim*, the stewards and watchers, God appointed us to be in Eden.

Watching is a time-related task; more than seeing and observing, it is guarding too. God does not want us to be complicit with Kronos through hasty action or through endless delay. We are to learn from the lessons of Elijah who waited so long to change the government as God had told him to, that he never completed it in his lifetime.

Naboth and his sons died as a consequence of Elijah's disobedience. Elisha was little better, though he did finally appoint one of the sons of the prophets—apparently Jonah—to complete the task of anointing Jehu.

Jonah of course is known for his refusal to heed God's call to preach at Nineveh; but it is likely he is the third generation of prophet to defy God.

Jesus, as the Healer of history and also the Author and Finisher of our faith, completes the governmental mandate that Elijah failed to fulfil—the sending out of a band of seventy to proclaim the coming of God. He also, through Peter's visit to Joppa, completed Jonah's mission to the Gentiles.

We are given grace in both its forms—unmerited favour and unstinting empowerment—to overcome the spirit of abuse and time. The Fruit of the Spirit, 'chesed'—*goodness, kindness, faithfulness*—is the weapon we need for this task. We also need to repent of our complicity with Time as the devourer of the future, whether that complicity is through dishonour of a Day that is significant to others, through beliefs about ourselves because of past abuse, through agreements about healing in relation to time, through self-sabotage on the threshold of our calling, through past participation in abortion, through delaying the appointment of those we know God has called to a particular position until it is too late—or through our family's involvement in any of these ways we can be allied with Time.

The grace of God is offered to us to change the future, bringing blessing to it, rather than allowing Kronos to devour it. Grumbling can cause us to be stuck in one place, unable to move on, while receiving continual retaliation for the dishonour we are speaking.

But it is up to us to ask God to break off our complicity and to annul all our covenants. We cannot do this ourselves, it is only through the power of the Cross of Jesus that it can be achieved. Throughout the process we need to act with honour, to say to Kronos, 'The Lord rebuke you!' and not assume we have the authority to do so while we still maintain allegiance to Time.

Immanuel, *God with us*, invites us to sit with Him in the eternal NOW of His presence. It is up to us whether we ask Him for the grace to take up the invitation.

Appendix 2

Additonal Prayers

A PRAYER FOR LOSS OF DESTINY BY SURVIVORS OF FAILED ABORTIONS:

Heavenly gracious Father, merciful God, I have made such a mess of my life. I am lost, lonely and alone. Nothing seems to go right. I feel unloved, even when Love embraces me. I feel that I have no right to exist. I want to hide, be invisible, be unnoticed—and at the same time, I want to be acknowledged, to be seen, to be wanted. I'm so confused, so muddled in my mind and spirit.

Will You come and breathe life into me? I know Your answer is *yes*, but I can't respond to it. I can't believe it. Please shine Your Christ-light into my life and show me Your love in the unique and particular way most needed by my heart. Lord, I acknowledge this way may not be what I believe is my greatest need, but I ask You to do so anyway. I also ask Jesus to grant me the ability to recognise this gift is from You and to help me open my spirit to You.

Lord, I know I don't understand life. It's so hard to accept, so challenging to welcome the life You chose for me. I invite You, Jesus, into my heart. I ask You to enfold me, close to Your own heart, to hide me under the wings of Your prayer shawl.

I ask You, Father, to forgive me for the choices I've made and help me forgive others for the choices imposed on me. Save and heal me, Lord. I want to come into full alignment with You and Your destiny for me but I can't do it, unless You guide me into it and encourage me every step of the way. I give my life and my destiny to You, Jesus, Father God and Holy Spirit, and ask all of You to cleanse the memories of my heart, wash the memories of my gut free of trauma, calm the memories of my mind and also fill my spirit with a knowledge of Your love and acceptance of me.

I choose to learn to love You. Please draw me into Your forgiveness, love and mercy, and hide me in Your arms of protection until I am not only safe but I feel safe. I hand over to You, Jesus, my control and my power to fulfill all Your purposes in and through me in Your perfect timing.

I ask this in Your name. Amen.

A Prayer to Accomplish Forgiveness by Survivors of Failed Abortions:

Heavenly gracious Father, merciful God and forgiving Lord, You love me. You love my mother and my father. You love all the people, some of them known to me, some unknown, who tried to take my life before it had ever really started. It's hard for me to see them with Your love but I want to choose to love the way You do. I therefore ask Jesus to mediate for me and, through the power of His blood, to activate my words. I can choose to say the words, Father, even though it is hard to feel the forgiveness. Yet I ask Jesus to manifest His forgiveness and unite them to my words.

I forgive my mother, my father, their parents, any of my family members, any of my parents' friends, associates or influencers who were instrumental in persuading my mother to choose to attempt to bring my life to an end even before I was born. I ask You, Lord, to empower these words to achieve the purpose You want for them.

Help me also, Lord Jesus, to see Your hand in rescuing and saving me from untimely death. I ask You to save others who, like me, find the feeling of forgiveness so difficult. Bring life into the desolate places within each of us. Bless all those millions of children cradled in wombs of terror and death. I ask You to protect all newly conceived babies from the enemy of life, and draw them all lovingly into Your arms.

You died for my sins and my wrong choices too, Lord. Forgive those who have aborted their little babies, and bring them all—the lost children, the mothers, those who survived the abortion attempt—safely to You, to know Your peace and Your love in all situations in their different griefs and losses.

Help me, Lord, to come fully into Your destiny for me and love others to life in You.

        In Jesus' name and in His cradle of love. Amen.

A Prayer to Seek Forgiveness for an Abortion:

Father God, I come to You and ask Your forgiveness for my abortion. I have killed my baby, an irreplaceable child who bore Your image, a unique person who had a calling and a destiny to complete. Your Word tells me You will forgive me when I come to You and ask. Sometimes I feel I can never forgive myself, but who am I to argue with You? If You say I am forgiven, then it is done.

Lord, I am truly sorry, I repent of my action and ask for the power of the Cross of Jesus to empower my words so a true turning is achieved and Your peace is a constant presence in my life. Lord, I have so little peace. I haven't known peace, except for fleeting moments, but now I look to You for peace. I ask Your forgiveness for my wrong thinking, for not trusting You, for listening to the advice of others and following the way of the world.

I ask Your forgiveness for the lies and rationalisations about abortion I have come to believe. I ask Your forgiveness for going my own way and not following You. I ask Your forgiveness for giving in to the pressure of those I allowed to take authority in my life.

I forgive those who manipulated and lied to me, who encouraged fear instead of faith, who coerced me despite my doubts, who weren't there for me when I needed them. I ask You, Jesus, to also empower these words of forgiveness and to realign my belief system with Your truth.

You were there, Lord, with my little one; You chose to be present and watch over my baby. I name my baby .... and I thank You for choosing my baby for Yourself and taking my little one into Your safekeeping.

Father, when this happened, I was overcome with fear and loneliness. I was without You. I felt powerless. Help me to know You, to experience Your peace, and to run to You when I am afraid and lonely, not try to cope on my own. I ask You to switch on my conscience, so I may understand Your Word.

Jesus, as Lord of the womb and as El Shaddai, the strong nurturer, I ask You cleanse my reproductive organs, especially from any spirits of death, murder, violence, rejection, abandonment and fear.

Please forgive me for the way I've sabotaged my own destiny through the lies I've believed and through the loss the person I was created to be. Restore me, Father, to my rightful design as I choose life in Your Son, Jesus Christ.

In His name. Amen.

A Prayer for the World:

Father, I ask You to rebuke the spirit of Death that has built a stronghold in so many nations and states around the world. I ask You to rebuke the enemy and to cut off all power, both spiritual and material, including financial, to those who feed on human sacrifice and on exploitation of every kind.

Maranatha! Come, Lord Jesus, and bring holiness to Your beloved people. Fill this world with Your love that is beyond comprehension and Your peace that passes all understanding. Teach us to hear Your still, small voice and to act in obedience to You. Grow the Fruit of the Spirit in us so that we can resist the assaults of the enemy—mature in us love, joy, peace, patience, kindness, goodness, faithfulness, gentleness, self-control. Grant us, as You promised, Your strength for the day.

Father, You so loved the world that You gave Your only Son for us so that whoever believes in Him will not perish but have eternal life. Help us to recognise and be ready for Your appointed times. Draw us close into You so we may know the all-encompassing warmth of Your forgiveness and how deeply You cherish each one of us and how You long to lavish us with blessings that overflow morning and evening, day after day.

In Jesus' name. Amen.

Endnotes

1. This translation comes from *An Australian Prayer Book*, Broughton Publishing 1978.

2. A 'throne guardian' is an ancient term referring to the officials of a king who are responsible for protecting the royal space surrounding his person and within his court. When 'throne guardian' is applied to God, it means His angelic courtiers: the four-faced cherubim who power His throne as well as the six-winged seraphim who are responsible for guarding the sanctity of sacred space—both in heaven and in its earthly counterpart, the Tabernacle.

3. See: rcm-usa.org/PDF%20Files/Cosmic%20Hierarchy%20and%20Appeal%202008-02.pdf (accessed 10 January 2021)

4. Habakkuk 3:5

5. For example Resheph, the seraph who in so many translations is reduced to a pile of hot coals or a puff of fiery sparks, is a stickler for honour towards God. As noted in *Dealing with Resheph*, it is instantly on the job and retaliates straight away when anyone approaches the altar of incense and dishonours God in prayer. *Dealing with Resheph: Spirit of Trouble, Strategies for the Threshold #6*, Armour Books 2020

6. Deuteronomy 32:8

7. 366 of these instances are 'ha'elohim', *the elohim*, and 7 are 'weha'elohim', *and the elohim*.

8. 'The simple meaning of Elohim here is "God," but many Second Temple readers understood *elohim* here as angels, as a Second Temple audience would not believe that a human being could walk with God Himself in heaven.' See thetorah.com/article/the-benei-elohim-the-watchers-and-the-origins-of-evil (accessed 31 May 2022)

9. 'Jesus, son of Sira begins and ends his panygeric of the patriarchs (44–50) with Enoch. Both Hebrew (MS B) and Greek texts state that Enoch walked with "the Lord," interpreting *ha-'elohîm* as God and not "the angels," as in other Enochic traditions. It tersely states that he was "removed" or "taken." The Hebrew version (MS B) states that this was a "sign of knowledge for generation after generation," and also states that Enoch was "perfect." The Greek version states that this was "a sign of repentance for the generations." These two differing views of Enoch are interesting to note.' hansmoscicke.wordpress.com/2017/09/25/enoch-mediatorial-tradition-a-brief-overview-part-1/ (accessed 2 May 2022)

10. Psalm 78:25 NIV

11. Enoch, after all, was considered to have talked and walked with angels. So it's not as 'far out' a concept as we would like to think for Abraham to done similarly.

12. Whether Gerar would have been considered a 'nation' in its own right in those days, with its own angel principality, is a difficult question. The nations of today obviously bear no resemblance to those of the past.

13. Scripture itself is unclear on how many days, but the most common suggestion is three. I've chosen *six* because that is the standard time between name covenants and threshold covenants elsewhere in the Bible. See: *God's Pageantry: The Threshold Guardians and the Covenant Defender,* Armour Books 2015.

14. These words were repeated a generation later when Abimelech tackled Isaac in an eerily similar situation. In my view, because of Abraham's repeated failure to pass the test when it came to trusting God's covenantal protection when he went with his wife to a foreign country, it became generational iniquity involving deception. Isaac was presented with an almost identical test and also failed. The test then twisted but still involved wives and

deception but, in the third generation, it turned around. Jacob was deceived when he unknowingly married Leah instead of the bride he had served for—Rachel.

15. *'Thus says the Lord: "If you can break My covenant with the day and My covenant with the night, so that day and night will not come at their appointed time, then also My covenant with David My servant may be broken, so that he shall not have a son to reign on his throne, and My covenant with the Levitical priests My ministers. As the host of heaven cannot be numbered and the sands of the sea cannot be measured, so I will multiply the offspring of David My servant, and the Levitical priests who minister to Me."'* Jeremiah 33:20–22 ESV

16. 2 Kings 18:15–16

17. See map at: alchetron.com/Valley-of-Rephaim (accessed 18 March 2022)

18. 2 Kings 18:17 NASB

19. Exodus 15:3 KJV

20. Based on the comments of Herodotus about the disaster that befell the Assyrians in Egypt, it is thought a similar event may have happened to the Assyrians outside Jerusalem. On Egypt he mentions: 'During the night a horde of field mice gnawed quivers and their bows and the handles of shields, with the result that many were killed, fleeing unarmed the next day.' Herodotus 2.141 See: haaretz.com/archaeology/2018-04-18/ty-article-magazine/.premium/how-mice-may-have-saved-jerusalem-2-700-years-ago-from- the-assyrians/00000 17f-e980-dea7-adff-f9fbfd210000 (Accessed 9 June 2022) A mice plague killing so many over several weeks is not implausible, but overnight seems highly unlikely.

21. yod-mem, 'yam', *sea;* and yod-vav-mem, 'yom', *day*. See also for the Sea-Day connection, Job 3:8 which is variously translated:

> *'Let those curse it who curse the Sea, those who are skilled to rouse up Leviathan.'* (NRS)
>
> *'Let those curse it who curse the day, who are skilled in rousing up Leviathan.'* (AMP)

22. Other threshold guardians are also evident in this story. See in this series: *Dealing with Leviathan: Spirit of Retaliation, Strategies for the Threshold* #5, Armour Books 2020

23. Not the innkeeper of Jericho, but the spirit that is often associated with 'Egypt' as a national entity.

24. It was excessively tempting and I only *just* restrained myself from mentioning the term, 'The Great Reset', in the text and instead restricting myself to this endnote. But from the basic principles in this book, I hope you can work out what the World Economic Forum's 'Great Reset' is counterfeiting.

25. See: https://www.randomgroovybiblefacts.com/up-a-tree.html (accessed 24 June 2022)

26. See Acts 14:8–18

27. See regarding dishonour of self, *Dealing with Leviathan: Spirit of Retaliation, Strategies for the Threshold* #5, Armour Books 2020. See regarding complicity with worthlessness, *Dealing with Belial: Spirit of Armies and Abuse, Strategies for the Threshold* #8, Armour Books 2022.

28. See in this series: *Name Covenant: Invitation to Friendship, Strategies for the Threshold* #3, Armour Books 2018

29. It should also be pointed out that much of Isaac's life is characterised by disputes and that his name sounds like 'esek', *dispute*. These disputes are with his neighbours, between his sons and, of course, the inheritance dispute that saw his half-brother exiled from home. Little wonder there is a dispute over birthright between his twin sons. The ancient principle of encoding of identity and destiny

in a name is not primarily etymological in nature, but poetic. Therefore rhymes, assonances and other lyrical devices, including puns and wordplay, should not be discounted. Features like 'esek' and 'Isaac' nevertheless tend to be entirely dismissed within the analytic framework favoured today.

30. ancient-origins.net/ancient-places-africa/baal-hammon-and-tanit-0012136 (accessed 13 June 2022)

31. christiananswers.net/dictionary/baal-hamon.html (accessed 12 June 2022)

32. That 'city' is the ever-burgeoning metropolis of the underworld ruled by the spirits of Death and Sheol. See: *Dealing with Resheph: Spirit of Trouble, Strategies for the Threshold* #6, Armour Books 2020

33. Joshua 19:28

34. See, however, the discussion in *God's Pageantry* regarding the problems with deciphering the name Abraham. The element 'hm' means *multitude*, but the issue is that the element is actually 'rhm' which does not exist in the Hebrew language. *God's Pageantry: The Threshold Guardians and the Covenant Defender*, Armour Books 2015

35. Derek Gilbert in *The Second Coming of Saturn: The Great Conjunction, America's Temple, and the Return of the Watchers,* Defender 2021, also identifies this entity as the Hurrian godling, Kumarbi; the Canaanite bull-god, El (not to be confused with 'el' as a word for 'God'); the Mesopotamian godling, Enlil; and also Dagan, the fish-grain godling of the Philistines, Akkadians and Amorites. These names do not include the various identifications for the leader of the Watchers other than Belial: Sahjaza, Semihazah, Shemihazah, Shemyazaz, Shemyaza, Sêmîazâz, Semjâzâ, Samjâzâ, Semhazah as well as, occasionally, Azazel and Gog.

36. Beck, the layout designer of this book, on reading this section offered a wonderful insight that I can't resist sharing:

'Coming from a farming town, I think the ram may also represent *fatherhood*. We expect to see a sacrificial lamb—a ram-son for a man-son—but instead, Abraham is presented with a ram, a father of lambs. In this scene, besides all the other things God is doing, He may be showing Abraham that He understands the nature of fatherhood, and what it is to have a precious son. God the Father knows the time will come when His own Son will be offered up as a sacrifice—in this very same place thousands of years hence. He may be demonstrating to Abraham, and to the Son Himself, that whatever agonies the Son must suffer, the Father partakes in, for the Father and Son are one. As the Son will suffer as God-with-us, human, the Father may suffer as God-above-us.

Why didn't Abraham bargain for the privilege of taking Isaac's place, as the ram stood in for the lamb? Was it his dearly-loved child on the altar, or merely his posterity? A person, or a promise? Yet the appearance of the ram underscores God's intimate knowledge of Abraham. In Ephesians 3 we learn that all fatherhood in heaven and on earth derives its name from God the Father. Abraham has borne not one, but two father-names—but the ultimate father is shown to be God.'

37. Luke 23:44

38. Luke 16:9; Luke 22:32

39. Daniel 7:19 NIV

40. Daniel 7:22 NIV

41. See: Derek Gilbert, *The Second Coming of Saturn: The Great Conjunction, America's Temple, and the Return of the Watchers*, Defender 2021

42. See: theoi.com/Protogenos/Khronos.html (accessed 30 January 2022)

43. He later describes them slightly differently: *'Each one had four faces: the first face was that of a cherub, the second*

that of a man, the third that of a lion, and the fourth that of an eagle.' Ezekiel 10:14 HCSB

44. That's 41.2 trillion km or 25.6 trillion miles.

45. See for more details: *God's Pottery: The Sea of Names and the Pierced Inheritance*, Armour Books 2016

46. R. Loren Sandford, *A Season of Tens: The move of God in the Millennium,* Exanimo Publishing 2000

47. This pattern showing the theme of hypocrisy running through these chapters is basically a summary of the teaching of Al Houghton on this topic.

48. Michael Heiser in his supernatural thriller, *Portent* (Façade Saga #2), a fictional vehicle for much theological exposition, points out that 'titan' also means *grey*. He explains this as a homograph, two words spelled exactly the same way but which are completely unrelated and have entirely different meanings. For a less technical word, try 'pun'.

49. See *Dealing with Belial: Spirit of Armies and Abuse, Strategies for the Threshold* #8, Armour Books 2022

50. 2 Kings 9:26 reveals the sons were murdered too.

51. Based on the length of Ahab's reign, Ahaziah's reign and Joram's reign, and also assuming that:

   (a) it was at least one year into Ahab's reign before Elijah delivered his announcement of the three and a half year drought

   (b) the two wars mentioned in 1 Kings 20 were in separate years

   (c) three years of peace were followed by a war in the fourth year

then it has to have been somewhere between 21 and 37 years after God told Elijah to anoint Jehu that one of the sons of the prophets finally declared Jehu to be king. Although Elisha went to Damascus, met Hazael and told him he would be king, there is no mention that he anointed him.

52. The gardeners paid what seems to have been a trespass offering for the use of the sacred streams of sacrificial blood. See: Anneli Sinkko, *John 18-20 and the Garden Traditions: A Literary and Theological Reading*, academia.edu/26937043 (accessed 4 June 2021)

53. See: *God's Priority: World-mending and Generational Testing*, Armour Books 2017

54. See: chabad.org/library/article_cdo/aid/464003/jewish/End-of-the-House-of-Omri.htm (accessed 30 June 2022)

55. This spirit is also called Turel or Tamiel. See bookofenoch.com/wp-content/uploads/2021/02/book-of-enoch.pdf

56. It's unclear whether she taught humanity some arcane arts involving snakebite and heatstroke or whether she taught healing of these issues.

57. See: lifesitenews.com/news/breaking-new-study-finds-preborn-babies-may-feel-pain-in-the-first-trimeste/ (accessed 2 July 2022)

58. See for more details: *Jesus and the Healing of History* series, Armour Books. For the significance of the Emmaus story, see volume #3, *Silk Shadows, Rings of Gold*. For the background to the Sychar story, see volume #1, *Like Wildflowers, Suddenly*. And for Bethany-beyond-the-Jordan, see volume #4, *Where His Feet Pass*.

59. You may wonder why I've included Jesus in this list and claimed that the mantle passed from John the Baptist to Him before He passed it on to Peter. The reason is because Jesus, as the 'Author and Finisher of our faith', clearly completes the governmental mandate that Elijah was given but did not bring to completion. This task was to send out band of seventy believers, spreading the good news of Yahweh's blessings to the villages of Samaria.

In addition, there are many more parallels between Jesus and Elijah than exist between John the Baptist and Elijah. John was the designated Elijah-who-was-to-come, as both the angel Gabriel and Jesus testified, and he began the work prophesied by Malachi of turning the hearts of children towards their fathers, but he did not complete it.

Jesus certainly lacked the 'Elijah look' that was a feature of John's appearance—the hairy garment and the leather belt—but, that aside, there are many aspects of his life and ministry that echo Elijah's. These parallels include:

- Jesus was carried up to heaven, just as Elijah was. Jesus was obscured by cloud and Elijah by a chariot of fire.

- Jesus went up a high mountain to challenge the 'Divine Assembly'—where Baal ruled and the 'sons of Asherah' held court. Elijah went up Mount Carmel and challenged the prophets of Baal and also the prophets of Asherah. Fire descended from heaven at Elijah's words; while a cloud of glory descended on Jesus.

- Elijah was faced with perversity, rejection and panic after he came down the mountain and heard Jezebel's threat. Jesus was faced with perversity and rejection after He came down the mountain.

- Jesus went to the region of Tyre and Sidon, and helped a woman and her child. Elijah went to the same region, and helped a widow and her child.

- Both Jesus and Elijah bring a widow's son back to life.

- Both of them prophesy before rulers and both of them call for repentance.

- Both of Elijah and Jesus hid in the Brook Cherith. Elijah hid in the Brook Cherith when his life was threatened by Ahab; in the last winter of His life Jesus hid out at Bethany-beyond-the-Jordan when His life was threatened.

- Both of them both encountered birds at the Brook Cherith. This was the place of Jesus' baptism—where His cousin John began his ministry. Here a dove rested on Him at the Lord's direction. Here in the days of Elijah, ravens provided food at the Lord's direction.

- Jesus fasted forty days in the wilderness after being driven from the Brook Cherith by the Holy Spirit. Afterwards He was ministered to by angels. Elijah, driven by Jezebel's threats, fasted forty days through the wilderness on his way to Mount Horeb, having been ministered to by an angel on the way.

- Jesus experienced three temptations in the wilderness. Elijah experienced three demonstrations of power in the wilderness—wind, earthquake, fire.

- The transfer to their successors involved a sign of fire. Elisha witnessed a chariot of fire as Elijah's mantle fell to him. The Holy Spirit came as tongues of fire to the disciples, led by Peter, at Pentecost.

- One of the last actions of both Jesus and Elijah involved the number 153. There were 153 fish caught in a net on the third occasion that Jesus appeared to His disciples after the resurrection. Just before Elijah goes on his last journey, three groups of fifty men led by a captain are sent by King Ahaziah to bring Elijah to him. The first two groups are destroyed by a firefall from heaven. The total of the three groups is 153 men.

60. Acts 10:15 NIV

61. Matthew 8:10 NIV

If you found this book helpful, other books in this series may prove useful too as you address the issues that bar your way into your calling:

Dealing with Python:

Spirit of Constriction

Strategies for the Threshold #1

On the threshold into your unique calling in life a dark spiritual sentinel waits. Scripture names it 'Python'—it has a God-given right to be there and test your significant choices. Trying to cast it out of a situation is useless.

Paul encountered it just as the Gospel was transitioning across a major threshold: the watershed moment when Christianity moved from Asia to Europe.

This book explores the tactics of Python, as well as its agenda. It offers insight into what this spirit hopes to get out of you and how you can rectify past mistakes involving this constricting, cunning enemy.

Dealing with Ziz:
Spirit of Forgetting

Strategies for the Threshold #2

The most significant threshold point of life is the doorway into God's unique calling for us. He invites us through covenant to fulfil the destiny we were born to achieve.

However, many of us fall at the threshold, rather than pass over it. We experience constriction, wasting, retaliation and forgetting—to such a degree it's easy to doubt the promises of God.

Dealing with Ziz examines the spiritual implications of forgetting in relation to threshold covenants. Since the opposite of remembering is dismembering—dismembering of truth—the spirit of forgetting is able to block access to our calling.

Yet there is an answer, a Fruit of the Spirit that overcomes Ziz.

Name Covenant:

Invitation to Friendship

Strategies for the Threshold #3

Abram became Abraham. Jacob became Israel. Simon beame Peter.

Name covenanting seems at first like an archaic, long-discarded practice that disappeared in the first century around the time Saul became Paul. The patriarchs and apostles exchanged names and so received new destinies. But that was then. And this is now.

However name covenanting never went away.

Robert Louis Stevenson became Teriitera. Paul Gauguin became Tioka. James Cook became Terreeoboo. Arthur Phillip became Woollaraarre.

These recent examples throw light on this ancient practice of friendship and kinship. They show us that, when God offers a new name, more than simply a new calling is attached. It's an invitation to friendship with Him.

If you're wondering how to overcome the issues of the threshold and the associated ungodly covenants, this book has the answer. Other books help you recognise the problem, this one points out the first step on the path.

Hidden in the Cleft:
True and False Refuge

Strategies for the Threshold #4

Jesus had a refuge—a safe haven—He retreated to when His life was in danger.

What does His choice reveal about where best to find sanctuary in times of trouble? What is the significance of the hiding place He used for an entire season? How can we discern the difference between a true and false refuge?

Removal of our false refuges is the first step towards achieving our life's calling—the divine purpose for which God created us. Yet all too often we fail to recognise how we've defaulted to a false refuge when disappointment strikes.

This book offers practical help, hope and encouragement towards achieving your destiny in Christ.

Dealing with Leviathan:

Spirit of Retaliation

Strategies for the Threshold #5

Retaliation, reprisal, retribution—many of us express the ferocity of our encounters with the spirit of Leviathan with such words. Most believers are stunned by savagery of the backlash they experience, and are baffled by God's seeming failure to intervene.

Reparation, recompense, restitution, restoration—these promised corrections to injustice are smashed just as they seem within reach. Why does this happen?

As we examine Scripture, we find that Leviathan is an officer of God's royal court. When we violate the consecration of that Holy Place, it has the legal right to remove us. It does not do so gently.

Dealing with Leviathan offers insight into overcoming this spirit of the deep.

Dealing with Resheph:
Spirit of Trouble

Strategies for the Threshold #6

Resheph is mentioned seven times in Scripture. A fallen seraph and throne guardian, it is identified here as a hidden face of Leviathan, the spirit that counterattacks against dishonour. Symbolised as a stag and an archer, Resheph is connected with flames and fire, fever, financial distress, mental illness, drought and scorching heat as well as the underworld.

Jesus warred against this spirit at least seven times. It's easy to miss these battles because it's easy to miss the prophecies Jesus was fulfilling and the mention of Resheph associated with them.

This is a companion volume to *Dealing With Leviathan* and examines the obstacles we face on the threshold into our calling.

Dealing with Azazel:

Spirit of Rejection

Strategies for the Threshold #7

'I am your only friend.'

That's the playbook line that works so superbly for the spirit of rejection. Most of us fall for it without ever realising our coping mechanisms—fight, flight, freeze, flatter, forestall or forget—are actually undermining our every effort to overcome this entity. So how can we subdue the spirit of rejection in our lives without sabotaging ourselves in the process?

This seventh book in the series, *Strategies for the Threshold*, addresses the nature of the spirit, its wider agenda, its spiritual legal rights, and its propensity for following after us to undo the good that we do.

Dealing with Belial:
Spirit of Armies and Abuse

Strategies for the Threshold #8

'What harmony,' Paul asked, *'is there between Christ and Belial?'*

Where, you might wonder, did he pluck that name from? In most English Bibles, it appears for the first time in Paul's second letter to the Corinthians. So it comes as a surprise to realise this army commander of the spirit world is mentioned 27 times in Hebrew, almost always in connection with abuse and violence. Modern translations generally substitute *worthless*. Yet from the stories where Belial appears, we can draw important principles for dealing with its tactics, agenda and ploys.

This eighth book in the series, *Strategies for the Threshold*, examines the spiritual dynamics involved in approaching your life's calling.

www.ingramcontent.com/pod-product-compliance
Lightning Source LLC
Chambersburg PA
CBHW021833110526
R18278200001B/R182782PG44588CBX00011B/17